CLEARLY ART
PILCHUCK'S GLASS LEGACY

LLOYD E. HERMAN

INTRODUCTION BY DALE CHIHULY

WHATCOM MUSEUM OF HISTORY & ART

1992

This book was published in connection with an exhibition and national tour prepared by the Whatcom Museum of History and Art, entitled CLEARLY ART: PILCHUCK'S GLASS LEGACY. The exhibition and publication were supported by grants from the National Endowment for the Arts, a federal agency; the Corning Foundation; the Washington State Arts Commission; the Art Alliance for Contemporary Glass; and Patrick and Darle Maveety.

Coordinated by John Olbrantz

Designed by W. Joseph Gagnon

Edited by Lane Morgan and Miriam Roberts

Typeset by Thomas and Kennedy

Printed and bound in Hong Kong through Interprint

Front cover: The Pilchuck Glass School, Stanwood, Washington.

Library of Congress Cataloguing-in-Publication Data

Herman, Lloyd E.
 Clearly art, Pilchuck's glass legacy/Lloyd E. Herman. p. cm.
 "Published in connection with an exhibition and national tour prepared by the Whatcom Museum of History and Art entitled Clearly art"—Verso t.p.
 Includes bibliographical references.
 ISBN 0-938506-00-5 : $19.95
 1. Glassware— Washington (State)—History—20th century—Exhibitions. 2. Pilchuck School—Alumni—Exhibitions. I. Whatcom Museum of History and Art. II. Title.
NK5112.H38 1992
748.2917 '71—dc20   92-81428
                                              CIP

Table of Contents

Preface

Glass as a medium has been one of a number of art forms experiencing renewed interest and technical "rediscovery" in the 1960's. This interest paralleled and was related to the growth of university art departments where facilities and technologies previously available only for factory production in ceramics, bronze, or glass were reinterpreted in a scale accessible to individual artists or their studios. The relationship of this transformation as applies to glass is exemplified and documented in *Clearly Art: Pilchuck's Glass Legacy.* For artists continuing to work in glass the Pilchuck School has emerged as the nation's major center of creative interaction and development. Over a twenty-year period the work of its participants, whether teachers or students, has had increasing recognition. After all this attention it seemed timely to provide an historical overview.

We are indebted to the efforts of Lloyd Herman in curating the exhibit and to John Olbrantz for its organization and catalog. We are most grateful to the many artists and lenders who have entrusted us with fragile art works for a three-year national tour.

The Whatcom Museum is pleased to present this first critical look at the work of artists associated with the Pilchuck School. For us it represents a way to share with a national audience the exciting growth of the Pilchuck School's influence. As a near neighbor in Northwest Washington, we have watched the development of the school with interest and, over the years, have worked with a number of the artists associated with Pilchuck. The close access to the artists, founders, and supporters of Pilchuck offered a special opportunity for a significant exhibit. Having now presented the exhibit and tour we are certain that those who see it will share our excitement.

George E. Thomas
Director
Whatcom Museum of History & Art

2

◁ **The central campus at Pilchuck.**

Acknowledgments

Artists, especially in Europe, have a long tradition of working with glass. However, until the early 1960s, the vast majority of blown glass was still made in factories. Few individual artists had access to the necessary equipment.

In 1962, at two workshops in Toledo, Ohio, Harvey K. Littleton, an associate professor of ceramics at the University of Wisconsin, and Dominick Labino, an inventor and glass chemist, designed and built a small furnace that would allow artists to blow glass in their studios. From their makeshift glassblowing facility behind the Toledo Museum of Art, Littleton and Labino would revolutionize the field of glass and usher in the studio glass movement in this country and abroad.

One of Littleton's first students in studio glass was Dale Chihuly, a native of Tacoma, Washington. While working as a glass instructor at the Rhode Island School of Design in 1970, Chihuly conceived of a summer glass school in a beautiful, wooded setting. His model was based on the Haystack Mountain School of Crafts on Deer Isle, Maine, where he had taught in 1968.

In 1971, with the financial support of Seattle art patrons John Hauberg and Anne Gould Hauberg, Chihuly founded the Pilchuck Glass School near Stanwood, Washington on a tree farm owned by the Haubergs. With limited financial resources but unlimited creative energy, the school took hold of a movement barely out of its infancy and propelled it to increasingly higher levels of artistic sophistication and technical innovation. In the short span of twenty years, Pilchuck has become synonymous with the growth and development of the studio glass movement in the United States and abroad.

Clearly Art: Pilchuck's Glass Legacy has been a project that I've wanted to implement for a number of years. The idea for the exhibition was born in the early 1980s at Dale Chihuly's studio in Seattle, where I listened intently as Dale told me about Pilchuck and its rustic origins. As I listened to him talk, it occurred to me that Pilchuck was truly a magical place where glass artists from around the globe could come to teach, share, experiment, and grow. I decided at the time that a history of Pilchuck was a wonderful and important story to tell, and I'm delighted that the exhibition, publication, and national tour have finally come to fruition.

As anyone involved in Pilchuck knows, teamwork is a critical element in the glassblowing process. Similarly, a project of this magnitude would not have been possible without the help of a number of creative and talented individuals, and I would like to take this opportunity to thank them for their commitment and support.

I would like to express my thanks and appreciation to the Board of Directors of the Whatcom Museum of History and Art in general, and Director George Thomas in particular, for their ongoing support of major exhibitions and publications of contemporary art. I am further indebted to a number of staff members for their time and help during the planning and implementation stages of the project: Michael Jacobsen, Exhibits Designer; Curt Mahle, Exhibits/Maintenance Assistant; Cathy Westfeldt, Exhibits Registrar; Mike Vouri, Public Affairs Officer; Gladys Fullford, Office Manager; Patrick Dowling, Custodian; and Julie Hadley, Museum Secretary.

When it was determined that we would proceed with the Pilchuck exhibition, I decided to contact Lloyd Herman, a curator and writer who lives in Bellingham, about his willingness to participate in the project. As the former Director of the

◁ **Student cottages at Pilchuck.**

4

Renwick Gallery in Washington, DC and one of the foremost authorities on contemporary crafts in the United States, I felt he would be an excellent choice to select the objects in the exhibition and write the essay for the book. My hunch proved accurate. His thoughtful selection of objects in the exhibition, coupled with his highly readable and informative essay, are destined to make a significant contribution to contemporary glass scholarship. I am further indebted to Lane Morgan and Miriam Roberts for their careful editing of Mr. Herman's essay, and to Joseph Gagnon for his beautiful design of the Pilchuck book.

I would like to extend a special thanks to the Board of Trustees and staff of the Pilchuck Glass School for making their records and photo archives available to Mr. Herman and the Whatcom Museum of History and Art staff, and Kate Elliott— former Pilchuck student and glass artist— for her time and help with the exhibition and publication.

Clearly Art: Pilchuck's Glass Legacy was supported, in part, by grants from the National Endowment for the Arts, a federal agency; the Corning Foundation; and the Washington State Arts Commission. In addition, the book received further support from the Art Alliance for Contemporary Glass and Patrick and Darle Maveety, and I am most grateful to them for their belief in our ability to carry out such an ambitious and, at times, overwhelming project.

I would like to express my thanks and appreciation to the many artists and lenders who agreed to part with their precious objects for an extensive national tour, and for their willingness to share their objects with audiences throughout the United States. I am further indebted to the many organizations— from New Hampshire to California—who have agreed to book the exhibition on its national tour.

Finally, and by no means least, I would like to thank John Hauberg and Anne Gould Hauberg for their ongoing leadership and financial support of Pilchuck over the past twenty years, and Dale Chihuly, whose vision and drive have transformed his dream of an atelier in the woods, devoted exclusively to glass, into a reality.

5

John Olbrantz
Deputy Director
Whatcom Museum of History & Art

▷ **William Morris, top right, and his crew.**

Foreword

Thirty years ago, in 1962, an extraordinary experiment in Toledo, Ohio, introduced a new medium to America's visual artists—glass. In 1971, in the foothills of the Cascade Mountains fifty miles north of Seattle, another experiment gave birth to an equally extraordinary art school —the Pilchuck Glass School. Today, twenty-one years after it was founded, Pilchuck is known to artists and collectors around the world as the international center of education for art in glass.

Nearly every significant artist using glass in America, and many from abroad, have taught in the school's fifteen-week summer program. They and their students from around the world return home from Pilchuck each summer physically exhausted but brimming with creative energy and ideas. The knowledge they have gained and friendships they have made will propel them forward as professionals. Pilchuck also has nurtured the recognition of glass art in the Puget Sound region, attracting an estimated 180 glassworkers to live and work in the area.

Today, at least two students apply for every vacancy in each of five sessions—in 1991 as many as eighty-seven applicants for some classes— and the school's annual budget exceeds one million dollars. It might be tempting merely to repeat a successful formula, refined over two decades, but the dynamic nature of the institution and its programs resist easy repetition. The school is the artists, their personalities, and their individual artistic contributions. The careful selection of each session's faculty and teaching assistants helps to ensure lively interaction and instruction.

Clearly Art: Pilchuck's Glass Legacy traces the school's development from its rustic origin as a one-summer experiment in communal living and art education in the woods. The exhibition features works made by a sampling of faculty members and visiting artists in Pilchuck's first twenty years. The objects show the wide range of aesthetic responses to a single medium and demonstrate the diverse glass processes the school has taught over the past two decades. They also illustrate the parallel growth of artistic sophistication and technical virtuosity and variety that characterize studio glass today. Certainly there are many more artists than are represented here who have served significantly as instructors, staff members, teaching assistants, and artists-in-residence in the twenty-one years since the school was founded. This selection does not diminish their contributions as teachers, or as artists, or their place in the art history of the late twentieth century.

I am grateful to those individuals who have been associated with Pilchuck over the years for permitting me to interview them, and to the school's founders, trustees, and staff for their generous help and advice.

Lloyd E. Herman

8

◁ **The Pilchuck lodge.**

Introduction

The origins of Pilchuck can be traced back to 1968, when I went to Maine for the summer to teach glassblowing at Haystack. Hidden away on a sleepy little island, the Haystack Mountain School of Crafts was a very special, almost magical place. I was completely taken with everything about it—the salty air, the moss-covered woods, the clean coastal light. I was especially taken by Fran Merritt, the school's founder. Inspired by this one-off visionary, this big-hearted Maine-iac, that summer I started to dream about creating a Pacific Coast equivalent to Haystack.

The dream crystallized further at the Rhode Island School of Design, where I'd been hired in the fall of 1969 to start up a glass department. At RISD I concocted a simple but effective teaching philosophy: motivate students to work *hard,* to immerse themselves totally in the medium, and interesting—sometimes even astonishing—results would inevitably follow. If students could spend enough time with the glass, I knew their talent would ultimately surface. Instead of handing out assignments along conventional lines, I asked them to come up with projects and ideas of their own. Then I let them develop the skills necessary to execute their personal vision by having them work alongside the most accomplished visiting artists I could find. And lo and behold, this somewhat unorthodox teaching method—a variation on the classic atelier model—seemed to work. Of course, with students as gung ho as Jamie Carpenter, Dan Dailey, Therman Statom, and Toots Zynsky, it would have been pretty hard for things to go wrong. Therman, for instance, bribed the night guards to let us keep the hot shop lit 24 hours a day, seven days a week. Those first months at RISD amounted to the most creative, highly charged institutional experience I'd ever been a part of. The energy flying around the place was enough to make your head spin.

In many ways RISD was the antitheses of bucolic, isolated Haystack. The setting in Rhode Island was anything but sheltered. We were right in the thick of the social and political ferment that was starting to rock the nation in the late 1960s, and it was kind of intoxicating. To protest escalation of the Vietnam War, we staged demonstrations that shut down RISD. During the downtime that resulted from this strike, a graduate student named John Landon and I began to talk seriously about starting a glass school. The right location, we knew, was crucial. Right from the get go, I never even considered situating it outside the borders of Washington State. The temperate Northwest climate was perfect, and we liked the idea of art students hitting the road and heading West to work in a rugged new landscape.

Our vision of a glass school was nudged abruptly toward reality when, in 1971, the Union of Independent Colleges of Art awarded my colleague Ruth Tamura and me a $2,000 grant. Our project was considered highly irregular, if not outright crazy. Part of our proposal was to allow sixteen gifted art students, two from each of the eight art schools in the UICA consortium, to come to Pilchuck free of charge for the summer.

My good friend Art Wood, a master graphic artist, designed a recruiting poster for us. In the imagined setting for the school that flowed from Art's pen, huge Douglas firs stood above the waters of Puget Sound, with the craggy, glaciated summits of the Cascade Range towering in the distance. Below the seductive landscape was a line of type that probably should have given applicants pause: "Recipients are to meet at Dale's mom's house in Tacoma, Washington." The bald

◁ **Inside the flat glass shop.**

truth was that as the weeks ticked down to Pilchuck's first session, we still didn't have a clue where the school was going to be.

Shortly after the poster was distributed, textile designer Jack Lenor Larsen—a colleague of mine at the University of Washington—introduced me to John and Anne Hauberg, art patrons from Seattle who were renowned for their generosity. The Haubergs said they had a site that might be suitable for our purpose—an abandoned barn, farmhouse, and outbuildings on a corner of a tree farm they owned fifty miles north of Seattle. They called the place Pilchuck, after the river Pilchuck that flowed through the property.

A couple of days before the sixteen students who were to make up the school's inaugural class showed up at my mom's home, Landon and I got our first look at the tree farm. The Haubergs had assumed we would want to make use of their empty buildings, but Landon and I were immediately drawn to a different part of the property, a hilltop clearing that had a commanding view of Puget Sound and the Skagit River Valley. Unfortunately this hilltop, with which we'd fallen hopelessly in love, had nothing on it but a bunch of cows—no buildings, no electricity, no utilities of any kind.

As insane as it probably seemed to people more rational than us, we decided we would rather build Pilchuck from scratch than move into the existing, less spectacular, site. I guess there's something to be said for being young and impulsive and more than a little bit crazy.

I hastily wrote, and then hand-delivered a letter to John Hauberg, asking him to drive up to the tree farm and discuss letting us use the new site we'd discovered. Despite the impracticality of the location, I felt very, very strongly that this mountaintop, with its striking views down to saltwater and beyond, was where the school should be. John, no doubt sensing the depth of my conviction, responded immediately. After walking back and forth across the hill, Hauberg, Landon, and I agreed that the Pilchuck hot shop should be built on the site where it stands today.

Dale Chihuly and Jamie Carpenter building the first hot glass shop, 1971.

Jamie Carpenter and Bob Hendrickson, ace woodsmen and builders, arrived a few days later. Construction began at a breakneck pace. At the same time, the students began appearing in Tacoma at my mom's. She bedded them down, fed them, and then sent them north by bus. As soon as they arrived at Pilchuck, the students were handed tools and told they would be building their own living quarters. In the interest of having a dry place to sleep, most of them went right to work. For my part, I took up residence in a 1970 Dodge truck. Landon erected a Sioux teepee on "Inspiration Point," and Jamie Carpenter, after salvaging some discarded windows, built a house out of glass. Pete "Kansas City" Robinson lived with his girlfriend in a hollowed-out, 14-foot-wide cedar tree trunk.

We discovered that one of the students, a guy from Seattle named Jonathan Block, had a knack with the telephone, so right away we set him up in a crude sort of office, where he became Pilchuck's version of Milo Minderbinder, scamming materials for the school with a zeal that was awesome to behold. A natural wheeler-dealer, Jonathan procured much of what we needed from government and Boeing surplus outlets; most of the rest came from thrift shops. Another student, Michael Norot, sewed the roof for our glass furnaces. I still have a vivid image of Michael, sitting on his butt in the tall grass of the hillside, stitching together

Dale Chihuly and Jamie Carpenter at Pilchuck, 1972.

11

Early Pilchuck faculty members. Left to right, Patrick Reyntiens, Italo Scanga, Dale Chihuly, Brian Clarke.

army-surplus tents to make a circus-style roof for the hot shop, which was the first thing we built.

Make no mistake: that first summer up there was a rough one—in some ways it was the worst summer I remember. But it was also the best summer I can remember. We worked like mad. Despite two straight weeks of nonstop rain, fourteen days after the students arrived we lit furnaces and blew the first piece of glass. The Haubergs were impressed by the determination we'd shown, and our willingness to suffer, I suppose, in the name of art. John was amazed that we'd built the hot shop so fast. Until then I think he'd considered us to be just a bunch of hippies, but from that point on both he and Anne took a keen interest in the school.

I was surprised at how quickly everything had fallen into place. Amid the frenzy, I realized that I was doing exactly what I wanted to be doing: blowing glass. My first installation at Pilchuck was a series of "floats" that I sent off like soap bubbles to sail in the pond behind the glass shop.

At RISD I'd learned that if you wanted to attract top-notch students, you needed to have a faculty of top-notch artists. Toward that end, Pilchuck invited a stream of distinguished artists-in-residence, including many painters and sculptors whose work had not previously been associated with glass. Pilchuck's facilities for working with molten glass succeeded in luring them from far and wide, because even though it was an ancient craft, in those days glassblowing was an almost entirely unexplored medium on the contemporary art scene. At Pilchuck, the artists-in-residence had the chance to see their wildest ideas given form by a team of glassblowers, which was a fairly unique opportunity. The notion of teamwork, by the way, was integral to my concept of the school.

Italo Scanga—my closest friend and mentor, a man known for his radical ideas —visited Pilchuck many times. I recall Italo coming into the hot shop and declaring, "I'm going to make glass with garlic." His plan was to pour molten glass onto the marveling table, put a garlic flower on top of it, and then quickly cover it with another puddle of molten glass. Presto!: the herb would blow a bubble as it gave off superheated garlic gas. Another time Jamie and I blew glass into a mold Italo had made out of bamboo. Needless to say, it burned up instantly, but I guess we succeeded in producing some sort of anti-Vietnam War statement.

The school hummed with a kind of manic energy in the early years. Right from the start, it also was imbued with a certain integrity—an integrity that stemmed in no small part from Italo's purity of vision. Among Italo's regular rantings and ravings, for example, he was often heard to proclaim, "There will be no giftshop bullshit at Pilchuck!" The school also managed to resist what might be described as the "craft mentality" and other subtle but tempting dangers, such as the commune ideology that was so much in vogue at the time. I felt it was important that distractions be kept to a minimum—I wanted every ounce of Pilchuck's energy to be focused intensely on the making of art.

At the conclusion of Pilchuck's first summer, John Hauberg came to me and asked how much we had overspent our original $2,000 grant. I candidly replied that the grant money had disappeared in the first week, and that I'd borrowed an additional $7,000 from a bank to cover the school's bills. Not only did John write a check to pay off that loan, he had grown sufficiently enamored of what we were doing up on his tree farm that he casually inquired what it would cost to keep Pilchuck running for a second summer. I told him it would be great to have a $25,000 annual budget. He agreed to foot the bill without batting an eye. And he continued to foot the bill for many years to come. Thanks in large part to John's uncommon generosity, Pilchuck not only survived but flourished. And for that, a whole lot of us are profoundly grateful.

Dale Chihuly

Dale Chihuly at Pilchuck, 1980.

John Landon's teepee, 1971.

Michael Norot sewing the roof of the first hot glass shop, 1971.

CLEARLY ART
PILCHUCK'S GLASS LEGACY

Introduction

Glass was hardly a new material for art in 1971, Pilchuck's first summer. Its aesthetic properties had been recognized in Egypt and Mesopotamia since the second millennium B.C.[1] Early in twentieth-century America the seductive luxury glass of Louis Comfort Tiffany and of Frederick Carder—founder of the Steuben Glass Works—was especially prized.

Tiffany and Carder, however, developed their creations with the help of skilled technicians in factories. Individual artists who wished to use glass as their medium had no way to melt and blow it in their studios. They had to find other ways to use the material. Clear or colored sheet glass could be composed into the leaded-glass pictures so familiar in church windows. Or it could be heated in a small kiln until soft and formed into shallow bowls, or fused in patterns to other sheet glass. It could be decorated with fired-on enamel, itself colored glass ground to fine powder. It could be engraved, faceted, sandblasted, and painted.

Traditional European techniques such as the cutting of crystal glassware were established in Seattle as early as 1912, when Czech immigrant Edward Zelasky established a business there. Anton Kusak, Sr., founded the Kusak Cut Glass Works in 1914, followed soon afterwards by the Kokesh Cut Glass studio. The latter two firms remain in operation today, run by the descendants of the original founders.[2]

Michael and Frances Higgins in Illinois gained recognition in the 1950s for their fused glass serving pieces and giftware, as did Maurice Heaton in New York State for enameled decoration on factory-made glass dishes. In Ohio, Edris Eckardt relied on her knowledge of ceramic glaze technology to develop her own methods of working glass. She formulated her own glass sheet or cullet, using a ceramics kiln, and progressed to working glass sculpturally, using the cire perdue technique in which crushed glass fills a mold and is heated until it fuses. When it cools, the resulting sculpture is removed.[3] In Washington State, Russell Day set chunks of colored glass into cement apertures to create glowing alternatives to conventional leaded glass windows.[4] It was a small field.

The breakthrough came in 1962 when Harvey K. Littleton, an associate professor of ceramics at the University of Wisconsin, and Dominick Labino, Vice President and Director of Research at Johns-Manville Glass Fiber Corporation, organized two experimental glass workshops at the Toledo Museum of Art. Littleton, whose father had been employed at the Corning Glass Works as Vice President and Director of Research, saw in glass a new artistic opportunity. Labino, an inventor and glass chemist—and an active member of the Toledo Area Artist Group—provided technical expertise, bringing glass marbles that would melt at the temperature achieved by the small furnace they developed together. In the fall following those workshops, Littleton founded the first university glass program in the United States, at the University of Wisconsin. His lectures and film presentations on blowing glass stimulated development of glass teaching programs in art schools and universities in other parts of the country.

The most important glassblowing demonstration that Littleton and Labino participated in occurred at the World Crafts Council Congress in New York City in 1964. Labino's innovative furnace—taken to the conference for participants to see—was eventually copied by new glass programs in several schools, further expanding the opportunity for individual work in glass.[5]

Dale Chihuly, a native of Tacoma, Washington, had experimented with

◁ **The lodge at Pilchuck.**

16

weaving glass strips into "window tapestries" while a student in the University of Washington's interior design program in the 1960s. Russell Day, who was a mentor to Chihuly, suggested Littleton's glass program,[6] and Jack Lenor Larsen, the internationally respected weaver and designer who had graduated from the UW design program years earlier, also urged him to go.[7] Upon graduation from the University of Washington in 1965, Chihuly enrolled. He finished Littleton's fledgling glass program in 1967 with an MS degree, and moved to Providence, Rhode Island, where he assisted Norman Schulman with his experimental glass program at the Rhode Island School of Design (RISD). There he earned an MFA degree in 1968 and was awarded a Tiffany Foundation grant and a Fulbright Fellowship to study glass in Italy—the first American glassblower to study in Venice.[8] After traveling throughout Europe in 1969 he returned to Providence to head the glass program at RISD. He taught there until 1979, when he was named Artist-in-Residence at the school.[9]

In 1968, Chihuly had accepted an invitation to teach at the Haystack Mountain School of Crafts on Deer Isle, Maine. His admiration for the school's director, Francis Merritt, its program, facilities, and its picturesque setting on the Maine coast fueled a new vision. Dale Chihuly's dream was to establish an atelier in a beautiful setting where students would come and work with a faculty of artists.[10] Haystack board member Jack Lenor Larsen encouraged that vision.

Chihuly's participation in the counterculture movement of the 1960s did not distract him from his goal, although it did influence his approach. "Dale and I were running the student strike at RISD shortly after the Cambodia offensive [in 1970]," his friend John Landon recalls. "During this period we sat down and Dale mentioned starting a glass school." [11]

Chihuly originally thought to have the summer program on a friend's property in Rosedale, Washington, across the Narrows Bridge from Tacoma.[12] Jack Lenor Larsen suggested that Chihuly talk to Seattle art patron John Hauberg. Larsen knew that John and his wife, Anne Gould Hauberg, owned a farm near Stanwood, Washington, fifty miles north of Seattle, which offered scenic beauty comparable to that of the Haystack school on the Maine coast. Chihuly was acquainted with Anne Gould Hauberg, to whom he once had given one of his "window tapestries." His phone call to her was a good opportunity to renew their acquaintance. The call led to a meeting, and a new location for the summer program was selected shortly thereafter. [13]

As John Hauberg recalls, Chihuly's proposal "was presented rather quickly and accepted rather quickly. Dale strode into our living room looking like an unmade bed—I was a bit shocked at this hippie—but he was proposing what Annie and I hoped we really could do.

"Dale simply said that he had been intrigued with the concept of the various disciplines of artists getting together for a summer of exchanging ideas, and in this case he had decided that the principal thrust this summer was to be glassblowing, but since everybody was to build his own house or shack and do his own cooking it would be something of a first." [14] Chihuly had encouraged a couple of architects and a photographer to come, as well as Landon, James Carpenter, and some other friends.

"Annie and I were very susceptible to the concept of this kind of thing taking

The first piece of glass blown at Pilchuck, 1971.

Glass Techniques

The aesthetic properties of glass have been valued for 4,000 years, and various methods have been used to form it in its molten state. Everyone has seen "glassblowers" at fairs and along seaside boardwalks, making crystalline filigree swans or sailing ships. That, however, is not truly glassblowing. It is lamp-working, so named because a rod of glass is heated over a "lamp," or bench burner, until the end is soft enough to stretch into threadlike strands for the creation of small figurines.

"Stained glass" is known to everyone for its use in church windows. Not usually "stained," such windows are composed of colored glass sheets, cut into patterns and joined with strips of lead or copper foil. Early leaded glass windows often have facial features or other details painted on the glass, too.

For glass to be blown, it is melted in a furnace to the consistency of thick syrup. A blow-pipe is dipped into the molten glass and, just as children blow soap bubbles, a gaffer (glass-blower) blows air into the glass to form a bubble. Though this is a simple description, the process is more complex and requires strength, skill, and control. Blowing glass is basic to the glass arts today, but until the early 1960s, furnaces to melt glass were found only in factories. Artists like Louis Comfort Tiffany directed skilled gaffers to blow vases or bowls to his specifications.

In 1962, a workshop at the Toledo Museum of Art introduced a glass cullet source that could be melted in a smaller furnace suitable for an artist's studio. Since that time glass-blowing has been the foundation of most glass art, and was the essential technique around which the Pilchuck Glass School was founded.

place on the tree farm," says Hauberg. "We had already had Henry Klein, an architect from Mount Vernon, draw up plans for a Mark Tobey museum on what we called Inspiration Point, a high bluff above where the school is now. We had taken this concept over to Basel [Switzerland] for Mark Tobey's okay, but he didn't like the idea at all. He didn't like anything being in the country. He hated the country. So there we were with a lot of ideas for using that beautiful site for something artistic. And nobody wanted to do anything about it until Dale showed up. So I fell into his idea very readily—in fact, immediately." [15]

John Landon recalls that "we looked at only two places—Paul Inveen's at Gig Harbor, then we met John [Hauberg] up at the ranch. We sat down and talked to John. The idea was very loose—we were just making it up as we went along; John probably knew that. That day John offered the white barn at the foot of the hill as a possibility. I remember that Dale and I walked around it, and it had a concrete floor and a roof and that was important. That night we showed Dale how to make a steak, throwing it right on the coals, and we discussed whether the white barn was what we wanted, but the next day we walked up the hill, up to the area by the pond, to Inspiration Point and to where the hot shop is now. There was this incredible view then, before the trees were so tall. Right there we kicked our heels in the dirt and said 'this is the spot.'" [16]

Chihuly recalls that in those days he always carried a typewriter, and that evening he sat down and wrote a letter to John Hauberg to confirm the proposal for the workshop's site. It was delivered by hand the following day and accepted. [17] John Hauberg agreed that it was a good choice: "We already had tree farm roads to that particular site and a fine pond so there was a water supply." [18]

Building the School

Prior to meeting with the Haubergs, Dale Chihuly and Ruth Tamura, Chairman of the Glass Department at the California College of Arts and Crafts, had been awarded a $2,000 grant from the Union of Independent Colleges of Art for an experimental two-month summer program in glass. Each of the eight member schools (San Francisco Art Institute, California College of Arts and Crafts, Kansas City Art Institute, Minneapolis Institute of Art, Philadelphia College of Art, Cleveland Art Institute, Maryland College of Art, and Rhode Island School of Design) was invited to send two students. Most of them didn't have glass programs, so it was an opportunity for interested students to explore the medium. Tamura arranged for students from her school to receive three academic credits by paying fifty dollars.[1]

Although a poster was distributed to universities and art schools advertising the opportunity to spend the summer, it is doubtful that many of the students realized just what they had gotten into. The site was hardly a campus in any conventional sense. The Haubergs had purchased the eight-square-mile tree farm after the Second World War. It comprised high, rolling meadowland and second-growth trees overlooking the Skagit River delta, with lots of old cedar stumps. They had formulated early plans for a development which was to have included a Mark Tobey museum, a pre-Columbian museum, and a golf course among its amenities, but a recession had ruined their plans before more than a septic system had been completed.[2]

John Hauberg remembers the first summer's staff as an odd and enterprising collection of people, including Landon, whom he calls "the cowboy builder," and one of his employees who cut shingles out of downed logs. "So all of these people joined forces, the shake maker, the cowboy builder and these architects, and Dale and Jamie [Carpenter] and Jamie's girlfriend [Barbara Vaessen]. We had no idea who else was with Dale, except that he had a small grant. And so we were quite surprised when a bunch of people showed up. Fritz Dreisbach showed up with a van that was a typical hippie production. He had his sleeping bag and facilities for cooking, and a complete hi-fi that could blow cows out of a field a mile away by cranking up the volume. There was hair all over the place—it was really something!"[3]

"It was the Woodstock of Glass!" said John Landon. "In fact one of the first-year people was at Woodstock; Buster [Simpson] helped with the sets!"[4] And indeed the first encampment, and the summer workshop's organization—or lack of it— had more to do with counterculture idealism of the 1960s than with formalized education.

First priority for each of the sixteen first-summer students was to design and build a shelter. Some scavenged local junk yards for cast-off building materials from which to construct a shack. John Landon made an Indian-style teepee. Another dug a hole to sleep in. Chihuly lived in his van the first summer. Three shelters constructed over the first three years—by Chihuly, Simpson, and Carpenter—remain as a reminder of the Pilchuck Glass School's hand-made beginnings, and for their own unique artistry.

Richard Marquis, on a temporary appointment at the University of Washington to provide glass instruction in the Ceramics Department, had access to government surplus, including army tents and equipment.[5] Fritz Dreisbach arrived well

◁ The cold glass shop.

into the first summer. He recalls visiting junk yards every afternoon in Mount Vernon and Arlington in search of other usable materials with which to build or operate the school.[6] There was no heat other than the glass furnace (after it was constructed and operating), and no electricity the first summer. A stream provided water. Everyone was initially responsible for cooking his or her own meals, but several would occasionally join forces to share a meal. Until their various shelters were habitable, the group lived in a farmhouse and barn two miles down the road.[7]

"We all lived and camped down there and used the kitchen in a communal situation," said James Carpenter. "And gradually as things began to get into place with the studio, we each on our own started initiating setting up tents or teepees or whatever was needed. Bathroom facilities were just porta-cans, and showers [were taken] down at the house which was two miles away."[8]

"Early on we realized that we couldn't let people do their own cooking because we got so many cans and bottles all over the place," said Hauberg. "It was really a mess."[9]

While meeting basic needs was a high priority for both faculty and students, much of each day was spent building two propane-fired firebrick furnaces in which to melt glass. Amazingly enough, within two weeks of their encampment the first glass was blown—under an improvised canopy to keep out the rain. Hardly art, the organic-looking blue goblet was a Pilchuck first.

The first-year faculty represented diverse talents and approaches to art but typified what Chihuly believed—that you invite good artists to make art, and students will learn from them. In addition to artists experienced with glass—notably Tamura and James Carpenter, Chihuly's student at RISD—the initial faculty also included the late Art Wood, a puppeteer and RISD instructor in silkscreen techniques, and Buster Simpson, an environmental mixed-media artist who worked with photography and video and arrived late in the first summer. Carpenter, who was also Chihuly's artistic collaborator at the time, was there the first three years. Other "regulars" who returned again and again included Fritz Dreisbach and, a year or two later, Italo Scanga and Paul Marioni. As the first woman on the faculty, Tamura describes her role as "chief cook and bottle washer," cooking the occasional communal meal and taking care of much of the paperwork.[10] There was not another woman on the faculty until 1979, though women did come as teaching assistants and as students.

Tamura remembers that after the first furnace was constructed the faculty and students signed up for blowing time—two or three hours a day, several days a week. Colored glass rods needed to make colored glass for blowing were not yet available, so colors were limited to the clear, green, brown, blue, and purple that could be made with colored glass marbles or formulated with chemicals. Because of limited access to the furnace, faculty and students also focused on other media. Some students came from backgrounds in ceramics and jewelry, which allowed them to diversify their work.[11] Simpson recalls that they attempted raku-fired ceramics[12] and Art Wood encouraged all to help create puppet shows. Any remaining time not spent on construction projects could be spent walking in the woods and sketching.

For urbanites, the seemingly limitless space of the great outdoors was rejuvenating and stimulating. Landon and Simpson—a veteran Boy Scout—encouraged

Art Wood's poster for Pilchuck, ▷ 1971.

Early faculty members Ruth Tamura and Buster Simpson, 1971.

The first hot glass shop, 1972.

the NO DEPOSIT *lots of returns* GLASS *etc.* WORKSHOP

sponsored by Union of Independent Colleges of Art

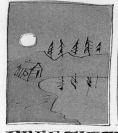

FREE TUITION – YOU PROVIDE FOOD AND CAMPING EQUIPMENT

SEE YOUR DEAN ABOUT PARTICULARS

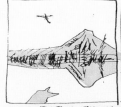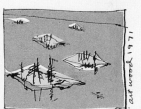

OR DALE CHIHULY AT RHODE ISLAND SCHOOL OF DESIGN, PROVIDENCE, R.I.

OR RUTH TAMURA AT CALIFORNIA COLLEGE OF ARTS AND CRAFTS AT OAKLAND

PUGET SOUND, STATE OF WASHINGTON JUNE 1ST AUGUST 1ST

VISITS TO OLYMPIC NATIONAL FORESTS, RAINFOREST, SAN JUAN ISLANDS, CASCADE MTS. MOUNT RAINIER, PACIFIC OCEAN, DALE'S MOTHER'S HOUSE

all to be aware of the environment they shared. Simpson remembers that some city dwellers were slow to learn the etiquette of camping in the woods. A fire that destroyed one of the living structures led to a centralized kitchen the second year, but the campers still provided their own fires for heat.[13] Though Simpson opposed the school's formalization as an institution at the time, he admits that "it was really much more efficient to have food prepared for people. It really was more efficient to have structures made…It was also safer."[14]

Notoriety came before respect. "Within three weeks [of the school's beginning]," John Hauberg recalls, "the local press had become aware of it, and the place was swarming with young reporters coming up there and bringing back tales both good and bad to the Everett and Stanwood papers and other local weeklies. Farmers were up in arms about those hippies up there smoking pot and so forth."[15]

Buster Simpson's tree house, 1973.

Some students were discouraged that they served primarily as a construction crew. It was hardly a comfortable summer outing; it rained most of the time, and keeping dry was a major concern. The glass furnaces truly became the "hearth" of the school, where everyone would come to warm up and dry off. The "peanut farm," as the school was called informally then, was an important experiment in communal living, but its growing pains began to point toward the need for more formal organization.

Tamura, in a report evaluating that first summer, recommended additions both to hygiene and to the curriculum. She suggested setting up showers near the toilets, which must have been a relief to the farmhouse tenants, and adding a second medium to the arts program.[16] She added that "everyone was glad that there was no tuition charge and felt that the workshop should be continued as a tuition free program."[17] That recommendation turned out to be infeasible, and a modest tuition charge was instituted the second year.

John Hauberg recalls that "at the end of the first year I went up the day everyone was leaving and we stood around in the rain, I think, and said 'Well, it was a good summer.' It was terribly wet and Dale said to me, 'John, what do you think about doing it again next summer?' and I said 'Fine with me.'"[18] And when Hauberg asked Chihuly "How much money do you need?" Chihuly replied, "$25,000." He got it.[19]

As souvenirs of that first summer Ruth Tamura and Buster Simpson cast bronze peanuts, improvising on the lost-wax method to remind those who were there of Anne Gould Hauberg's favorite name for the place.[20] But the "peanut farm" name gave way to Pilchuck Workshops by 1973, then Pilchuck Glass Center. The first official name, The Pilchuck School, was eventually changed in 1986 to the Pilchuck Glass School.[21] "Pilchuck" is a Northwest Indian word meaning "red river."[22]

During the second summer a large army tent provided shelter for a kitchen and pantry, and another served as a mess hall and a place to show slides with electricity provided by a generator. It rained most of that summer, too, but work progressed refining the facilities.

Kate Elliott, a student in 1972 who has since served the school in various professional capacities, recalls that the second year's program was advertised in a little newsletter circulated to a number of art schools and universities, and that recruitment required applicants for the summer program to send in some piece

23

Faculty and staff share a meal in the lodge dining room.

of art with the application, or a video or photographs. "All applications went to Dale at RISD. My guess is that he, and probably Jamie Carpenter, looked through the applications and picked a few from around the country so that they would spread the word. I paid $350 for the whole summer." [23]

The announcement did not adequately describe the school's primitive facilities. Therman Statom was a student the second year: "When I first came to Pilchuck I had just gotten out of high school and it was my first year working in glass, and I got to this place and expected to see this furnace. [What I discovered] was this cement pad—and logs. The first thing that struck me was 'where am I going to stay?' You had to build your own house! I built this really neat yurt, [and] we all built the furnaces together." [24]

The increasing number of furnaces afforded more blowing time for all. "There were less people [than today], and you had all summer," said Statom. "Time was not the issue; I think once I blew eighteen hours in one day—so much that I couldn't use my hands. The school was definitely a place where a person could go and come out different." [25]

James Carpenter returned from Italy that year and introduced a new tool, the marver—a smooth sheet of steel onto which a hot glass bubble may be rolled to create a shape or to "pick up" other colored glass chips or rods. The marver enabled artists to blow larger works. The second year also introduced the first faculty member from abroad, Erwin Eisch from Germany, who was known for his poetic imagery and remarkably expressive mold-blown heads and telephones. Eisch and other international glass artists had previously participated in workshops for Joel Philip Myers, at Illinois State University, Normal, and for Harvey Littleton at the University of Wisconsin. Marvin Lipofsky, hosting the Great California Glass Symposia at the University of California, Berkeley, and eventually at the California College of Arts and Crafts, from 1968 until 1986, also brought in international glass artists. Pilchuck was to build on these examples to become the center for international artistic communication in glass.

Although glass remained Pilchuck's focus the second summer, experiments went on in other media. "There were a lot of artists coming and going very informally," Statom recalls. "They would come and do a body of work, and do performances." [26]

In addition to Wood's puppet shows, faculty and students the second year created their own "happenings": Fritz Dreisbach pouring hot molten glass onto cold glass, slug races, and videotaped pieces such as one of lightweight sculptural forms being blown across the pond by wind. Attending as the wife of environmental/ephemeral artist Doug Hollis, Ruth Reichl, now food editor of the *Los Angeles Times,* got into the spirit of the place and cooked a breakfast on hot glass. [27]

John Hauberg remembers that "at the end of the second summer we stood around a little bit longer and said 'well, what do we need?' And at that point after two rainy summers we wanted to just get out of the rain! The hot shop was the result of that. And I told Dale at that point that I thought he was a fine leader of the art group but not a good administrator, and he practically kissed me! So I [eventually] got Mimi Pierce, who had been involved with Annie and me in Pacific Northwest Art Center efforts, and Mimi agreed to do the best she could." [28] She worked from 1974 to 1976, assisted in the day-to-day operation of the school by Rob Adamson, who later founded the Glass Eye, a glassblowing studio and retail outlet in Seattle.[29]

By the third summer, the faculty-student roles had become better defined, but there was a bit of anarchy as students began to complain that they had paid to be there and that they spent more time on construction projects and work teams than blowing glass. Richard Posner, a shop technician that year, says that a "Tom, Dick, Harry, and Mabel" rotation of jobs was used, and those with spouses or girlfriends had the benefit of sharing assignments, whether washing dishes, shopping for food or cleaning up after meals: "The democracy of it forced people to…pay attention to the banal details of living together, yet it afforded a way to interact with one another that the more traditional craft education didn't do," Posner said. "I mean, if Dale's premise for Pilchuck was based on Haystack, then I would think the other vision—whether it was Buster's or people like myself coming up there and projecting it onto the place—was more like a Black Mountain College."[30]

Black Mountain College, the experimental school in North Carolina—like Pilchuck, based in rural foothills—existed from the 1930s into the 1950s. It integrated various visual and performing arts disciplines, and was governed by whomever was there at the time, acting as faculty and/or students. Among the illustrious faculty were Joseph and Anni Albers, John Cage, Merce Cunningham, R. Buckminster Fuller, Karen Karnes, Robert Rauschenberg, and Peter Voulkos. Others at Pilchuck may have seen similarities between it and Black Mountain, but Chihuly denies that any schools other than Haystack and RISD inspired his vision.[31]

The hot shop building started in 1973 [and completed in 1974] was the first building designed by Thomas L. Bosworth, an architect on the University of Washington faculty whose course Anne Gould Hauberg had once audited. Buster Simpson recalls that ideas for future building were discussed that same year: "The basic floorplan of the main lodge was conceived, actually drawn out," said Simpson. "I remember sitting around at Jamie Carpenter's little house that he had there, with Dale and Jamie and I going over it…the two-sided fireplace, exterior stairways, how the lodge and the kitchen were oriented…"[32]

In 1974, Benjamin Moore began the first year of a thirteen-year stint in charge of education. Dan Dailey and Paul Marioni returned year after year to teach in the summer. Others, respected today as established artists, who came to the school through the years as teaching assistants to the faculty included Sonja Blomdahl, Robert Carlson, KeKe Cribbs, Stephen Dale Edwards, Walter Lieberman, Charles Parriott, Susan Stinsmuehlen-Amend, and Catherine "Cappy" Thompson. Many of them returned to the school to teach, as did former students Therman Statom and Toots Zynsky, among others. John Reed, who was a student at the school in the 1970s, has remained as Assistant Director for Campus Operations.

Though the summer program was growing into a more formal arts institution, the exploration of art and the environment remained informal and experimental. As earth-movers prepared to clear the site for the hot shop in 1973, Richard Posner staged a mock archeological dig, unearthing "Winston Pilchuck" tumblers with Winston Churchill's likeness that he had made and then buried.[33]

Other improvements included the hiring of full-time cooks [who were also

Building the School, 1971-77

During the nine years before the first Pilchuck summer in 1971, blown glass dominated the growing community of glass artists. Blown forms were joined together while hot to make new shapes, spread out to form shallow bowls, and pulled up to make tall vases. Many of the artists who came to Pilchuck as faculty members during the school's formative years, 1971-77, had progressed beyond the blown vessel. They brought a spirit of experimentation to the new program.

For example, Harvey Littleton had begun to develop sculptural forms and was experimenting with one of the "warm techniques"—slumping—in which glass sheets are heated until soft enough to be bent and then combined into sculpture, as shown in *Optic Wave*. Robert Naess was blowing glass into molds, sometimes combining such mold-shaped elements with flat glass and blown shapes incorporating murrini to make small sculptures that commented on the cold war with the Soviet Union. William Bernstein was drawing on hot glass vessels with clear glass threads. Robert Levin was blowing and shaping hot glass into cups shaped like bananas and such objects as *Specialty Item for Robbing a Fruit Stand*—a banana gun and holster with tiny slug-shaped bullets.

Pop Art was a phenomenon of the 1960s, and by the end of that decade we had seen popular imagery transformed into social and political protest art. In their sculpture, artists of the Funk Ceramic Movement—which began in the San Francisco Bay area—thumbed their nose at "The Establishment," perceived as government, big business, and most other institutions. It is not surprising that artists working in glass had caught the spirit of the times. Pilchuck was, after all, an art education and social living experiment outside the

degree-carrying artists] to release students to spend more time blowing glass, as well as refinement of the school's crude technical set-up. During Mimi Pierce's administration the full-summer session split into two sessions, then three, enabling the school to receive more money from tuition. Some students came on scholarships, often worked out with their own schools specifically for the program. In 1976, Pierce said approximately one-third of the students were artists working professionally in glass, one-third were university or art school graduates, and one-third were undergraduates—often with no experience with glass. "At Pilchuck everything is open," Pierce said. "There are always some people who come in with more technical knowledge than anyone else has and like to share it."[34]

Students were selected from applications including slides of their work, two letters of recommendation, and a statement of why they wanted to study at Pilchuck. Pierce said that "most of them say that it's because it's an intensive program and they've gone as far as they can in the program where they are, and they want to improve their skills and learn more about what is happening in glass."[35] Pierce's appointment enabled Chihuly to concentrate on the artistic development of the school, and he soon realized that good artists do not necessarily make good teachers. It would be necessary to begin choosing faculty members for their teaching skills and establish a more formalized system than his earlier dream of an atelier in the woods.

More international artists were invited to the faculty. Marvin Lipofsky and Richard Marquis, Americans who had visited Venetian glass factories, imparted their knowledge of Venetian filigree techniques. The introduction of such European techniques and the team approach to glassblowing were to become increasingly important to the school's growth in general and to Chihuly's own work in particular.

Harvey Littleton, founder of the studio glass movement in America, first taught at Pilchuck in 1974 but states that "my relationship to Pilchuck has always been one of a cheerleader... The great success of Pilchuck has been the enthusiasm and work that everyone contributed under Dale's leadership.

"I believe that the foreign visitors have gained much more from Pilchuck than they were able to contribute," says Littleton. "Most of the visitors brought skills and left with inspiration. There is only now [1991] beginning in Europe anything that approaches Pilchuck with the summer course at Frauenau started by Erwin Eisch called the Bildwerk, and he is happy to credit Pilchuck and his experience there."[36]

Though the Haubergs paid for the $30,000 hot shop, they did not view it as a long-term commitment to funding the summer education program. They merely believed that if better work was to be made in glass, better facilities had to be provided to make it possible. The Haubergs continued to be generous with their financial support and personal encouragement, but other sources began to provide modest support for the undertaking.

"The growth was very organic," John Hauberg recounts, "and the first three buildings I think I built with some grants. I think we got a grant from the Weyerhaeuser Foundation, and one from the Seattle Foundation for bricks and mortar. We managed to build, by 1977, four buildings. The first was the little latrine, which later became a photographic lab. Then the hot shop, the cold shop and the lodge, and the covered footbridge to it."[37]

Support in the form of equipment came from the Corning Glass Works, cullet from Seattle's Northwest Glass Company, and more and more financial help from the wider community as glass art became increasingly desirable to collect. The school also began to hold fundraising auctions of glass art donated by faculty and students.

Bosworth, architect of all ten of Pilchuck's buildings, succeeded Mimi Pierce as director in 1977. He presided over the completion of the flat glass shop during Pierce's last year as director and the entire construction of the lodge during his administration, ending in 1979. Describing his architectural approach to the site, Bosworth has written: "It seemed appropriate that the new buildings be rugged and simple, should become a part of the natural setting. Logs, heavy timbers, cedar siding and large-scale cedar shakes like those used on nineteenth-century rural buildings in Washington made sense, as did the sympathetic relationship between the land and barns and other rustic farm and forest outbuildings which are part of the architectural imagery of the Northwest."[38]

The Bosworth years at Pilchuck were characterized by stablization and growth. Though one faculty member lamented Bosworth's authoritarian manner, he nevertheless praised him for making the school professional. "Before that it was a hippie camp. He got money raised and channelled into more equipment, and good equipment. He got out brochures and publicity, and the place became a professional school because of Tom and Dale during that period."[39]

The first hot glass shop under construction, 1971. Dale Chihuly in center.

Inside Dale Chihuly's house, 1974. Left to right, Erica Friedman, Dale Chihuly, Italo Scanga.

▷**William Bernstein**
Fangs Battles Woman
1978
Blown glass with cane drawing
8 x 6 x 6″
Collection of Paul Marioni, Seattle, Washington

BUILDING THE SCHOOL

James Carpenter
Vase
1975
Blown and cast glass
11¼ x 8⅛ x 8⅛″
Courtesy of the Artist,
New York, New York

▷ Dale Chihuly
Blanket Cylinder
1975
Blown glass with applied
glass threads and powder
14½ x 8 x 7½″
Collection of George Stroemple,
Portland, Oregon

Dale Chihuly and
James Carpenter
Door
1973
Glass rondels, leaded blown
glass set in wood frame
86 x 41″
Collection of Dale Chihuly,
Seattle, Washington

BUILDING THE SCHOOL

Dan Dailey
Nail Vase N.9.76
1976
Irridized blown glass with steel
nails and cane decoration
11 x 5¼ x 5¼"
Collection of Daniel Greenberg
and Susan Steinhauser,
Los Angeles, California

▷ Marvin Lipofsky, with the assis-
tance of Gianni Toso
Split Piece, *from the Fratelli-
Toso Series*
1977-78
Blown, cut, and polished glass
with cane underlays
9 x 17 x 12," 6 x 11 x 11"
Collection of John H. Hauberg,
Seattle, Washington

Erwin Eisch
Telefon
1971
Mold-blown glass with
gold luster decoration
6¼ x 9 x 6¾"
Collection of Anne Gould
Hauberg, Seattle, Washington

▷ Harvey Littleton
Optic Wave
1978
Slumped optical glass
10½ x 32 x 18"
Collection of the Artist,
Spruce Pine, North Carolina

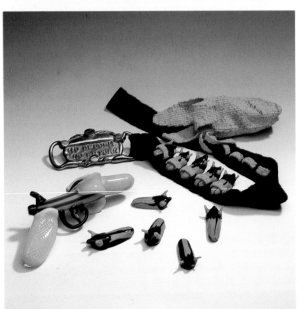

Robert Levin
**Specialty Item for Robbing
a Fruit Stand**
1975-76
Blown and molded glass,
woven wool
Belt: 1⅜ x 50⅜ x 4⅛"
Gun: 3⅝ x 11½ x 5⅜"
Collection of the
Lannan Foundation,
Los Angeles, California

BUILDING THE SCHOOL

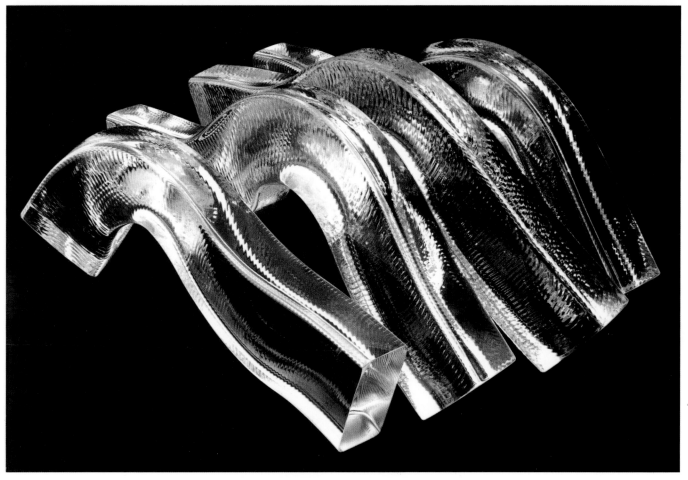

BUILDING THE SCHOOL

Paul Marioni
Plug—For Those Who Dare
1975
Leaded glass, cebatrans photo,
fired enamels
26 x 28'''
Courtesy of the Artist and the
William Traver Gallery,
Seattle, Washington

▷ Robert Naess
Political Nose Cup
1972
Blown glass with murrini
4⅛ x 5¼ x 2⅞"
Collection of
Robert L. Pfannebecker,
Lancaster, Pennsylvania

Jack Schmidt
Lottery Game #129
1972
Blown and mirrored glass,
acid-etched
6⅛ x 20 x 14"
Courtesy of the Artist,
Toledo, Ohio

BUILDING THE SCHOOL

Pilchuck and the World

Concentrating on the artistic direction of Pilchuck, Dale Chihuly continued experimenting with the make-up of faculty and session length. In 1978 the faculty expanded from an average of seven instructors to eleven, as more sessions were added and as planning for the present-day five-session summer formula was refined. In 1979 the faculty grew to twelve, and in 1980 to seventeen, plus two artists-in-residence. The faculty became more specifically glass artists, and then glass artists with teaching ability. Students during the school's first few summers had grown impatient with performing other duties that had prevented them from blowing glass; they had come for instruction and Chihuly knew that he had to supply it, although he continued to champion teachers who were also good artists, believing that he was designing an art school, not a summer crafts school like Haystack or the Penland School of Crafts in North Carolina. Some staff members became important teachers, their successful artistic careers indelibly linked to the school.

William Morris, for example, arrived in 1978 to work initially as a driver and laborer and became an expert gaffer with an expanding artistic vision.[1] Living at the school and using its facilities, he has also provided continuity through various staff changes as Assistant Artistic Director, working closely with Chihuly, and as Artistic Director until August 1991. Flora Mace came as Chihuly's teaching assistant in 1979 and with collaborator Joey Kirkpatrick built a cabin on Pilchuck property for their use until they established an independent studio in Seattle in the 1980s. Much of their art was made at Pilchuck, where they were the first artists-in-residence assistants.

The Artists-in-Residence program grew serendipitously. Initially, students lacked an opportunity to observe, and perhaps assist, artists making their own art. To fill this gap Chihuly invited one or two glass artists, who often arrived unannounced and were called Visiting Artists. One of the first in the formalized Artists-in-Residence program in 1980 was the Italian glass master, Lino Tagliapietra. In the eyes of many, Tagliapietra became the key figure in making available to artists Venetian filigree techniques that had been guarded for centuries. Therman Statom refers to Pilchuck's "school" style today as "West Coast/Italian."[2]

International faculty members grew in number. Ludwig Schaffrath taught from 1977 through 1980, the first of several German artists to introduce the possibility that leaded glass was appropriate to contemporary artistic expression, not just pictorial windows in the Tiffany style. Patrick Reyntiens brought his personal style in leaded glass from England, as did Brian Clarke.

German artist Klaus Moje and his wife, Isgard, came to teach in 1979. Since his acceptance of a teaching position in Australia in 1982, Moje has returned often to teach his methods of composing and laminating intricately patterned platters and bowls of cut and ground glass. Asked what international faculty members brought to the school, Moje replied that Europeans had the techniques, but Americans had the ideas. Each learned from the other.[3] It was often said during these years that Pilchuck was better known in Europe than it was in Seattle.[4]

Though the hot shop remained the heart of the school, the techniques taught there—and in the flat glass and cold shops—proliferated. Master engraver Jiří Harcuba and the remarkably gifted husband and wife team, Stanislav Libenský and Jaroslava Brychtová, whose angular cast sculptures had to be scaled down to

Faculty member Ginny Ruffner.

fit Pilchuck's annealing ovens, were among the first to arrive from Czechoslovakia. Another husband and wife, Bertil Vallien and Ulrica Hydman-Vallien, came from Sweden for several years, introducing sandcasting of molten glass and personal painted imagery, respectively, to their students and fellow faculty members. Sometimes artists from abroad taught and sometimes they were invited as artists-in-residence.

International students came too. By 1990 nearly one third of all students were from outside the United States, the largest number from Canada and Japan.[5] In some cases the students came to study with a faculty member from their own country who was otherwise inaccessible to them.

To attract faculty and students from abroad, an International Council was set up by the board in 1982-83, with Thomas S. Buechner of the Corning Museum of Glass as chair. Council members—chosen primarily from museums in several countries—secured some help with tuition expenses for students from their countries and, perhaps more important, represented the perspective of modern glass as art rather than decorative craft.[6]

In 1984 the Artists-in-Residence program began to include successful artists working in other media, such as Lynda Benglis and John Torreano, among others. It was a return to Chihuly's first-year vision of bringing differing artistic viewpoints and methods of working.

Artists-in-residence had no teaching responsibilities but were asked to give a slide talk about their work so that others at the school—both faculty and students—could see what they might have to share. There was a "carrot" for visiting artists: each was allotted so many hours of a skilled gaffer's time to blow objects for them. This encouraged them to examine glass as another material suitable for their art. Undoubtedly in Chihuly's mind was the possibility that artists from the "fine arts" who began to use glass would help to bring favorable attention to the medium.

Contemporary glass was beginning to earn the respect of the art world. Publications began to feature glass art and artists. An increasing number of museum exhibitions, along with the establishment of galleries devoted exclusively to contemporary glass, began to stimulate the interest of collectors. Objects by Thomas Patti, a young artist whose work was featured on the catalogue cover for the important international exhibition of contemporary glass organized by the Corning Museum of Glass in 1979, *New Glass,* were accepted into the prestigious collections of New York's Metropolitan Museum of Art and Museum of Modern Art. Chihuly's work gained widespread exposure through solo and group exhibitions in this country and abroad.

The material beauty of glass, to some artists, is a curse. Though it is immediately alluring even to the uninitiated in art, some artists and critics believe its glittering transparency competes with its potential for being taken seriously for artistic content. Chihuly's Artists-in-Residence program could introduce glass to those whose art was issue-oriented. By 1987 the faculty list included thirty-two instructors and eighteen artists-in-residence. Both groups included American and international artists, and artists-in-residence ranged from painters to video journalists.

Alice Rooney was hired in 1980 as Pilchuck's Executive Director after she had

Pilchuck and the World, 1978-91

Forming Glass

The school's enrollment grew when summers began to be divided into several sessions. Chihuly and the school's staff and faculty responded to every clue that students wanted more ways of manipulating glass. Many were eager to pursue perfection in blown forms, and teachers such as Sonja Blomdahl and Dante Marioni gave them more, demonstrating the importance of a unique color sensibility. Others wanted more than only blowing bubbles in glass; they wanted to learn forming techniques to create vessels and sculpture: *pate de verre* was taught by Diana Hobson from England, and Karla Trinkley, an American.

Bertil Vallien came from Sweden to introduce sandcasting. William Morris and others mastered mold blowing techniques and taught them to others. Slumping, fusing, and other "warm glass" techniques were taught by respected artists such as Klaus Moje and Mary Shaffer. Grinding, glueing, or fusing, and polishing glass into sculptural form was the forte of instructors such as William Carlson and David Huchthausen. Lampworking was renewed as a technique suitable for art by Ginny Ruffner and Susan Plum, and neon was introduced by artists such as Bill Concannon as another form of glass to be worked over a flame, adding light and color to sculptural shape.

Along with Howard Ben Tré, the revered Czechoslovakian artists Stanislav Libenský and his wife, Jaroslava Brychtová, introduced monumental cast sculpture, and a large annealing oven was constructed to accommodate their creations. But none of these processes replaced the sculptural techniques of working hot glass straight from the furnace; Fritz Dreisbach, Richard Marquis, William Morris, the renowned

Italian glass master Lino Taglia-pietra, and others continued to demonstrate that skill and taught it to their students. And Toots Zynsky, using equipment developed for her to extrude "spaghetti" of molten glass, continues to employ the process to layer glowing color in the bowls she forms.

Combining Techniques

Richard Marquis, the first American to develop and apply Venetian techniques—filigree work and the use of murrini—to his own unique style, has also influenced others by artistically combining materials and techniques. Many of the school's artists-in-residence have come from other art media to experiment with glass. Works by artists such as Lynda Benglis and John Torreano demonstrate their skill incorporating the special qualities of glass into their sculptures. The school provided skilled gaffers to blow shapes that the guest artists hoped to incorporate into their work.

served for twenty years as Executive Director of Allied Arts of Seattle. She was respected in the arts community as a sound administrator well acquainted with sources of funds. The right person at the right time, she enabled the school to grow into Dale Chihuly's expansive vision.

Since John Hauberg, who until Rooney's appointment had assumed the school's financial obligations not covered by tuition, had said it was time for the school to become more self-sustaining, it was clearly Rooney's role to enlarge the financial base. An early step was the establishment of the Pilchuck Society in 1980 to manage the school's first annual fund drive, which today raises over $200,000 a year.[7]

The school's board originally sprang from the same Pacific Northwest Art Center group that supplied Mimi Pierce. At the time the school was incorporated in 1976, the five-member board participated in deliberations of school matters but the important program decisions were made by the Haubergs and Chihuly.[8] In the early 1980s, Rooney and Hauberg reached beyond his Seattle coterie to attract prosperous businessmen with strong ties to philanthropic corporations, wealthy collectors, and community activists. The board grew to twenty-one members in the early 1980s and thirty-eight in 1992. Five glass artists, including Chihuly, were elected in 1991-92.[9]

Hauberg served as board president for ten years, after briefer terms held by two of his friends, Dr. Joseph McCarthy and Frank R. Kitchell. Since 1988, board presidents are elected to two-year terms. In addition to tapping a broader range of financial resources, the current board takes a more direct role in decisions concerning the school's function and direction.[10]

Commenting on her tenure as the school's executive director, 1980-90, Rooney has said:

I have always felt that the fundraising was obviously and simply a means to important goals. During my ten years at Pilchuck, I felt the challenge was in managing growth.

Beginning in 1981, the school had full enrollment, which meant different numbers as time went by as we increased capacity—housing, studio space, etc... We built ten buildings during those years. The administrative summer staffs doubled. The sessions increased from three to five per summer. Within each session, classes increased from three to five. Artists-in-residence not only increased from one to two artists, but included artists working in materials other than glass—i.e., sculptors, painters, printmakers, etc.

As non-glass artists, they needed more assistance than the glass artists who knew about blowing schedules, materials, kilns and annealers, etc. During my last summer, the print program began. My concern over the years was to protect the spirit of Pilchuck while at the same time making best and most efficient use of resources and providing for the safety and comfort of those in residence. It would have been easy to create a bureaucracy with a lot of rigid rules. I think we managed to deal with the growth and at the same time understand that Pilchuck is a place devoted to creativity and learning and is first and foremost the artist's place.[11]

During the 1980s, some colleges began to close down their glass programs because of mounting expenses, so Pilchuck became increasingly important as alternative education in the glass arts. Scholarships, funded by the school or by individual patrons or schools elsewhere, added to its appeal. Scholarships valued at more than $70,000 were awarded for the 1991 summer program.

Pilchuck also was more generous than summer craft schools in paying faculty and so was able to attract the best in the field, a fact lamented by Jack Lenor Larsen when he was chairman of the board at the Haystack Mountain School of Crafts and Pilchuck was new. He recalled that Pilchuck was paying several times what Haystack could afford.[12] Alice Rooney says that faculty pay at Pilchuck may have been greater but that the disparity was less than Larsen thought.[13] She did acknowledge that Pilchuck's greatest expenses are propane and people.

When Alice Rooney left the school in 1990, the annual budget exceeded $1 million—a four-fold growth in ten years—only forty percent of which was covered by tuition. Her departure as executive director, and Chihuly's as artistic director [he then joined the board], marked the end of an intense period of growth. John Hauberg, who is still an active member of the board, understands that the school, like virtually all arts institutions, can never cover expenses by fees charged to its users. He looks forward to establishing a national patrons group to broaden financial support to the school.

The appointment of Marjorie Levy as director in 1991, merging both administrative and artistic roles, should help to bring greater national and international attention to the school. She is an experienced artist [in clay], an academician [from the arts faculties of Purdue University and the University of Michigan, where she served as dean of the School of Art just prior to her Pilchuck appointment], and an articulate spokesperson who is able to build bridges between artistic and administrative concerns and people.

A sign of Pilchuck's more solidified role was the 1991 course, Masterpieces, which ventured officially into the history of glass. Chihuly, Richard Marquis, and Lino Tagliapietra joined glass historian William Warmus in examining historical objects made by the Egyptians, Romans, and Venetians, as well as by modern masters such as Galle and Carlo Scarpa. The artists explored how the ancient techniques can be adapted to contemporary artistic concerns. That course attracted established artists—themselves former Pilchuck faculty members—as students and teaching assistants. It also points to the future use of art history—especially in glass—to deepen the meaning of contemporary work and to encourage critical writing in the field.

Furthermore, over the years the school has responded to the expanding glass field by offering classes in such diverse processes as lampworking, neon, *pate de verre,* and various "warm" glassworking techniques such as slumping and fusing.

Today the school is at its maximum population of 100, and the site cannot sustain more. John Hauberg comments that there has already been some slight erosion on the hill. "We froze the concept by building the lodge with seating for meals for 100 people, so we are not interested in growing number-wise. We can extend the season, improve the equipment, etc., but we would hope not to build any more, although we do need twenty more beds up there."[14]

Half the hundred are faculty and staff, all artists, whatever their jobs. The equal ratio of faculty and staff to students is laudable, but it limits the number of students in five two-week sessions to only 250 per summer.

John Hauberg thinks that "this is absolutely great. Pilchuck should reach for

Flat Glass

The flat glass shop, completed in 1980, enabled the school to attract international artists of architectural glass to teach—Patrick Reyntiens from England, Ludwig Schaffrath and Johannes Schreiter from Germany, and Lutz Haufschild from Canada, among others. American artists introduced diverse ideas: Albinas Elskus demonstrated through his work that painting skills could also serve an artist composing art from flat glass panels; Susan Stinsmuehlen-Amend broke new ground with her mixed media constructions of juxtaposed colors and shapes that often shocked the visual senses. Others, like Henry Halem, developed personal style in creating collages of opaque colored glass, often embellishing its surface. Ed Carpenter team-taught with Tim O'Neill the considerations of using glass to modulate light in architectural installations.

▷ Faculty member Narcissus Quagliata.

quality, not quantity. If such a striving leads to exclusiveness or elitism, Pilchuck will have to be careful to be open to all and not become a club or clique. I think the board is very much aware of this."[15] To ensure that the board is responsive to artistic concerns, William Morris, Benjamin Moore, and Joey Kirkpatrick—all of whom are both the products of the school and leaders of its success—joined Ginny Ruffner and Chihuly as the first artist members of the board in 1991.

The school does continue to grow by extending its season. The Emerging-Artists-in-Residence program for less established artists began at the end of the summer sessions in 1990. Five emerging artists were chosen from applications. Each received a $1,000 stipend plus up to twelve weeks of housing at Pilchuck. They had use of all the facilities except the hot shop, and a technician was on hand to assist.

"Each made a body of work and it was fantastic," said Joey Kirkpatrick. She and Flora Mace initiated funding for the new program by adding an additional auction to the annual fundraising auction held at the end of each summer. "There was an additional auction to the fall affair, and artists donated work for the second time. Since we had already given we asked if we could get together as a group and talk about how we'd like to see this money used... For years Dale had wanted to get a fall program going, where artists could come and work, because the buildings were sitting there. And obviously it costs to heat them, etc., and we've been trying to figure that out for years, so we pigeon-holed some of the money that we raised from the auction for this program."[16]

The glass plate printmaking program begun in 1990 was another initiative from Pilchuck artist/donors and certain board members, and the sale of prints helps to sustain it.

Why has Pilchuck succeeded? What lies ahead for the school? What are the challenges to its future growth and its sustained popularity?

"Dale is never satisfied. He is always tinkering with the school to try to make it better," explains Thomas Buechner.[17]

James Carpenter elaborates. "Dale absolutely cannot be given enough credit for what he did on this—not just at Pilchuck, but his momentum and drive have quite literally built the entire glass movement."[18] Acknowledging Harvey Littleton's role in sending his students out into the world to teach and establish other glass teaching programs, Carpenter notes that Pilchuck "really attracts people from all over the world... He [Chihuly], in fact more than anyone, has created the market for selling glass. He, more than anyone else, has validated crossing the boundaries between art and craft and he, of course, must be given full credit for seeing this potential and almost being a one-man magnet—orchestrator— of all of these events."[19]

Pilchuck faces challenges, to be sure. Though this exhibition was organized twenty years after Pilchuck's first experimental summer and begins its national tour during the thirtieth anniversary of the studio glass movement in America, glass is hardly beyond its infancy as a medium for contemporary art. But it is not too much to expect full acceptance in the visual arts internationally in this century; after all, both printmaking and photography have transcended early identification as mere technical processes.

In 1991 the world grew smaller. Political walls disappeared, national identities

Embellishing the Glass Surface

Imagery on glass began to rival glass forming techniques in importance to the school's offerings. Cappy Thompson transferred her unique neo-medieval painting style from leaded-glass windows to three-dimensional bowls, painting images with enamel—ground glass in solution—that would be fired onto the glass surface. Dick Weiss, too, moved from windows to bowls. Both relied on skilled gaffers associated with the school—William Morris, Benjamin Moore, and Richard Royal—to blow their blanks. Robert Carlson and Walter Lieberman merged shape and image in their often-detailed scenes on glass.

European artists such as Erwin Eisch from Germany, Dana Záměčníková from Czechoslovakia, and Ulrica Hydman-Vallien and Ann Wolff from Sweden, shared their unique styles of narrative imagery in their sessions. And as Ann Wolff used acid-etching and sandblasting to lightly etch the surface of glass, Michael Glancy employed sandblasting to carve deeply the glass vessels he would then electroplate with metal. Master engraver Jiří Harcuba from Czechoslovakia demonstrated the application of his technique for portraits cut into glass disks.

Other artists were invited who preferred to explore painting on the flat surface, and for artists like Therman Statom there were flat surfaces on several dimensions. Works by Statom and flat glass artist Robert Kehlmann exemplify a gestural, abstract use of applied color. Judy Bally Jensen introduced the technique of reverse painting on glass to her Pilchuck students in 1991.

Though numerous teachers provided a range of artistic viewpoints about creating images on the glass surface, Chihuly's own use of Navajo blanket images fused onto the vessel surface—a glass thread technique that he developed at Pilchuck in 1974 with James Carpenter, Kate Elliott, and Italo Scanga—and Paul Marioni's exquisite use of integral narrative imagery, must not be overlooked. Likewise important is the contribution to glass art technique by Flora Mace and Joey Kirkpatrick, whose early figure drawings of wire fused to glass led to increasingly larger figurative sculpture made of mold-blown glass elements and other materials. That combination of materials was first introduced to Pilchuck by Italo Scanga, whose artistic freedom has inspired faculty and students over the years.

Glass Plate Prints

In 1990, artists donating work to the Pilchuck fundraising auction initiated a printmaking program at the school. Artists-in-residence, faculty, and staff were given the opportunity to paint, etch or sandblast images on glass plates which would be printed by pressing paper against the painted or inked plate. Painting the plate permits the printing of only one strong image—a monoprint—but occasionally the glass plate retains enough color to print a second "ghost print." Multiple images are possible with an etched and inked plate. Most artists consider their prints experimental, but those exhibited demonstrate the vitality of the art produced in the program.

Pilchuck faculty members and others have increased the vocabulary of glass processes that are now available to artists. By freeing their students to use whatever techniques suit their artistic concepts, they have moved glass to the forefront as a medium for art equal to all others.

>The Pilchuck Glass School sign.

were renewed, and communication improved among artists around the world. The Pilchuck Glass School has already demonstrated that glass can provide a universal language for artists of many nations. With the continuity of strong administrative and artistic leadership and the establishment of a sound financial base, Pilchuck will surely remain in the forefront in the new century.

PILCHUCK AND THE WORLD

Sonja Blomdahl
Apricot/Clear/Blue Green
1991
Blown glass
13 x 12 x 12"
Courtesy of the Artist and
the William Traver Gallery,
Seattle, Washington

Michael Glancy
Corinthian Star X
1984
**Blown and plate glass,
sandblasted and electro-
formed with copper**
8½ x 10 x 10"
Collection of Daniel Greenberg
and Susan Steinhauser,
Los Angeles, California

Dale Chihuly
White Sea Form Set
(not illustrated)
1985
Blown glass
29 x 32 x 18"
Courtesy of the Artist and
the Foster/White Gallery,
Seattle, Washington

Fritz Dreisbach
**Purple Mongo Vase with
Multi-hue Filigree, Three
Ferns and Cast Foot**
1990
Blown and cast glass
16 x 11 x 9½"
Courtesy of the Artist and
the William Traver Gallery,
Seattle, Washington

Flora C. Mace and
Joey Kirkpatrick
Acrobats
1983
**Blown glass with wire and
cane drawing**
10¼ x 7 x 7"
Collection of the Artists,
Seattle, Washington

VESSELS

Paul Marioni
Hot Nights
1988
Blown glass with colored glass
underlay
12¾ x 7 x 7″
Courtesy of the Artist and
the William Traver Gallery,
Seattle, Washington

▷ Dante Marioni
Whopper
1990
Blown glass
28 x 11 x 11″
Courtesy of the Artist and
the William Traver Gallery,
Seattle, Washington

Richard Marquis
Woody Goblet
1980
Blown, mold-blown, and
fabricated glass with murrini
6¼ x 8 x 4″
Collection of the Artist,
Freeland, Washington

45

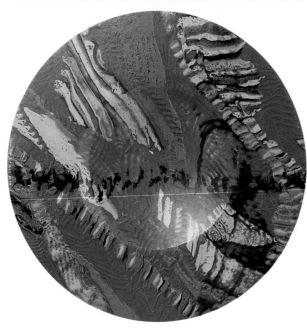

Klaus Moje
Untitled
1990
Kiln-formed mosaic glass,
slumped and wheel ground
2¾ x 21 x 21″
Collection of Sonny and Gloria
Kamm, Encino, California

VESSELS

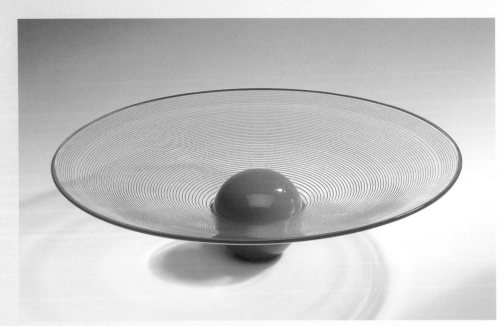

Benjamin Moore
Platter, *from the Palla Series*
1990
Blown glass
4 x 19 x 19″
Courtesy of the Artist and
the William Traver Gallery,
Seattle, Washington

VESSELS

William Morris
Stone Vessel *(not illustrated)*
1984
Blown glass with overlays
15 x 12 x 4½"
Collection of the Artist,
Arlington, Washington

▽Joel Philip Myers
CFBYELLKSG 19841
1984
Blown glass with applied shards
and glass threads, acid-etched
7¼ x 15 x 3¼"
Collection of Daniel Greenberg
and Susan Steinhauser,
Los Angeles, California

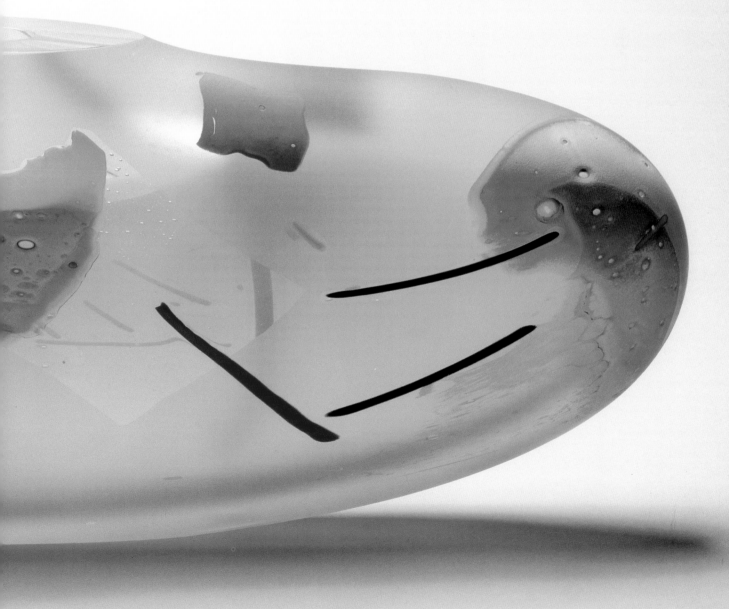

VESSELS

VESSELS

Danny Perkins
Fire House
1991
Blown glass, broken and
reassembled, oil paint
48 x 11 x 11″
Courtesy of the Artist and
the William Traver Gallery,
Seattle, Washington

Italo Scanga and Richard Royal
Untitled, *from the Bird*
Vase Series
1991
Blown and manipulated glass
with applied glass "jimmies"
23 x 15 x 11″
Courtesy of the Artists,
San Diego, California and
Seattle, Washington

Buster Simpson
Spring Goblets
1983
Manipulated glass, chromed
bedsprings
8 x 4 x 4″ each
Courtesy of the Artist,
Seattle, Washington

VESSELS

Lino Tagliapietra
Spirale
1991
Blown glass
29¼ x 4½ x 4½″
**Courtesy of the Artist and
the William Traver Gallery,
Seattle, Washington**

▷ Cappy Thompson, "blank"
blown by Tom Kreager
Adam Naming the Animals
1987
Blown glass, fired enamel
10 x 18 x 18″
**Collection of the Artist,
Seattle, Washington**

Dick Weiss, "blank" blown by
Benjamin Moore
June 24th
1990
Blown glass, fired enamels
18 x 11 x 11″
**Courtesy of the Artist and
the William Traver Gallery,
Seattle, Washington**

51

VESSELS

VESSELS

Ann Wolff
Untitled
1983
Blown overlaid glass,
sandblasted and acid-etched
8 x 9¼ x 9¼ "
Collection of Daniel Greenberg
and Susan Steinhauser,
Los Angeles, California

Toots Zynsky
Lavender/Amber/Black
1991
Fused glass fibers
7 x 12 x 7"
Courtesy of the Artist and the
Snyderman Gallery,
Philadelphia, Pennsylvania

▷**Howard Ben Tré**
Cast Form 68
1989
Cast glass, gold leaf, pigmented
waxes
36 x 7⅛ x 5¼"
Collection of Daniel Greenberg
and Susan Steinhauser,
Los Angeles, California

VESSELS

SCULPTURE

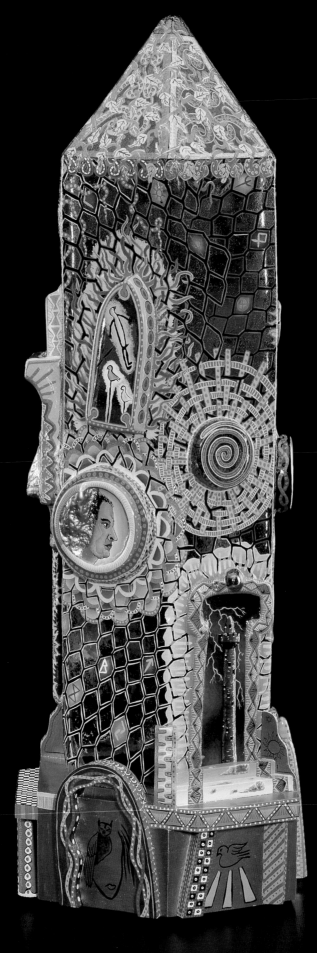

SCULPTURE

> Lynda Benglis
Zita
1984
Sandcast and manipulated
glass with copper and color
additions
8¾ x 11⅝ x 12¼″
Collection of Dorothy and
George Saxe,
Menlo Park, California

◁ Robert Carlson
Shiva's Net
1989
Blown glass, wood,
enamel paint
29 x 12 x 12″
Collection of John H. Hauberg,
Seattle, Washington

William Carlson
Contrapuntal
1992
Cast and laminated glass
and granite
26¾ x 16 x 5½″
Courtesy of the Artist,
Urbana, Illinois

SCULPTURE

Dale Chihuly
**Emerald Gold Venetian with
Three Stems**
1991
Blown glass
31 x 70 x 20″
Courtesy of the Artist and
the Foster/White Gallery,
Seattle, Washington

Dale Chihuly
**Venetian Drawing—NY Lino
Blow** (not illustrated)
1992
Acrylic and charcoal on paper
30 x 22″
Courtesy of the Artist and
the Foster/White Gallery,
Seattle, Washington

Bill Concannon
Honeymoon in Elko
1991
Neon, plastic, wood,
found objects
42 x 22 x 18″
Courtesy of the Artist and
the William Traver Gallery,
Seattle, Washington

Dan Dailey
Fatigue
1983
**Fabricated plate glass, Vitrolite,
nickel plated brass**
15 x 12 x 8″
Courtesy of the Artist and the
Kurland/Summers Gallery,
Los Angeles, California

SCULPTURE

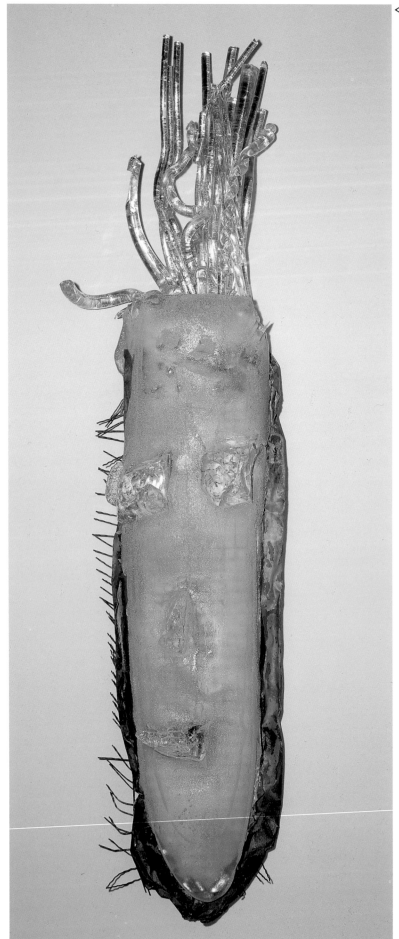

◁ Ann Gardner
Gold Face
1987
Sandcast glass, copper, acrylic paint
33 x 8 x 3"
Collection of Anne Gould Hauberg, Seattle, Washington

59

Jiří Harcuba ▷
Colette
1984
Engraved glass
5¾ x 5¾ x ¾"
Collection of Elly Sherman, Los Angeles, California

Jiří Harcuba
Colette *(not illustrated)*
1984
Graphite on paper
17 x 13¼"
Collection of Ruth T. Summers and Bruce W. Bowen, Los Angeles, California

SCULPTURE

SCULPTURE

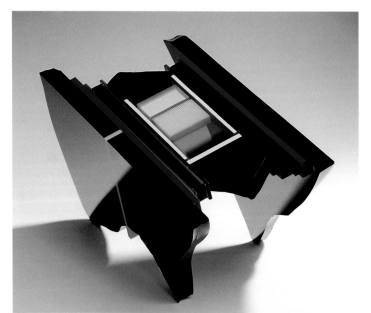

David Huchthausen
Leitungs Scherbe
1986
Fabricated, cut, and polished
glass
12 x 20 x 12″
Courtesy of the Artist and the
William Traver Gallery,
Seattle, Washington

Ulrica Hydman-Vallien
Thunder Vase
1990
Blown glass, fired enamels
8 x 17 x 17″
Collection of Herbert and
Lucy Pruzan, Mercer Island,
Washington

61

Margie Jervis and
Susie Krasnican
Three Vessels
1983
Plate glass, fired enamels
22 x 72 x 1½″
Collection of Kate Elliott,
Seattle, Washington

SCULPTURE

Stanislav Libenský and
Jaroslava Brychtová
Red Head
1990
Cast glass
31½ x 7 x 24½″
Courtesy of the Artists and the
Maurine Littleton Gallery,
Washington, DC

SCULPTURE

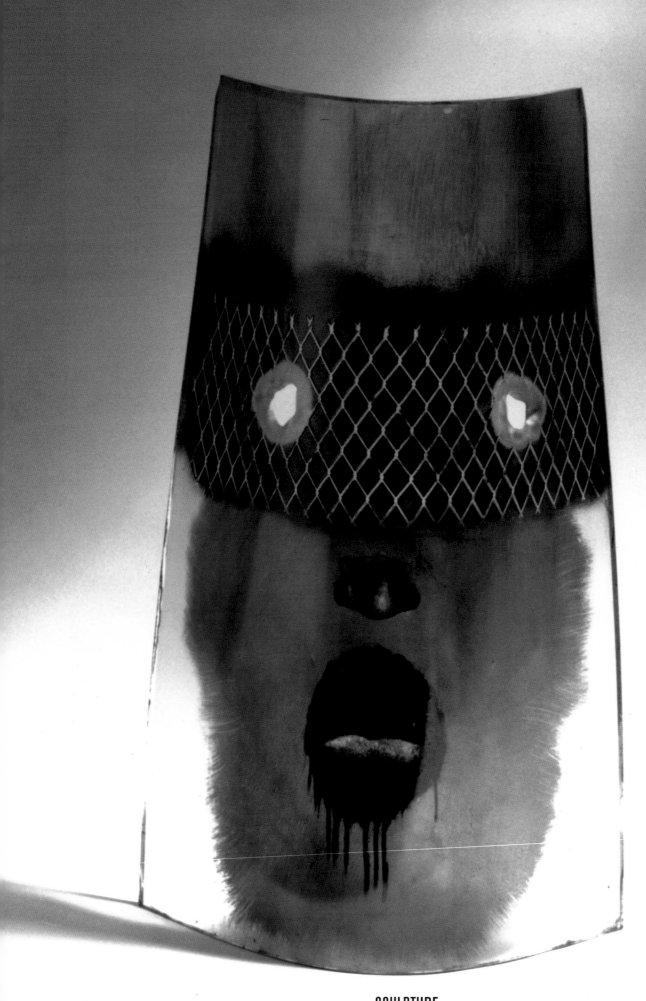

SCULPTURE

William Morris
Burial Raft
1991
Blown and manipulated glass,
painted steel stand
10½ x 21 x 10"
Courtesy of the Artist and
the Foster/White Gallery,
Seattle, Washington

Dennis Oppenheim
Bee Hive Volcano
1979-89
Blown glass, tape player,
soundtrack
18 x 12 x 12" each
Courtesy of the Artist and
Blum Helman Gallery,
New York, New York

Flora C. Mace and
Joey Kirkpatrick
Seasons Continuance
(not illustrated)
1989
Blown and painted glass, wood
24 x 32 x 15"
Courtesy of the Artists,
Seattle, Washington

◁ Walter Lieberman
Prisoner of Conscience
1986
Enameled and sandblasted glass
24 x 14½ x 5½"
Collection of Bill and
Anne Traver,
Seattle, Washington

Richard Marquis
Bubble Boy *(not illustrated)*
1988
Blown and fabricated glass,
enamel paint
30 x 19 x 11"
Collection of the Artist,
Freeland, Washington

SCULPTURE

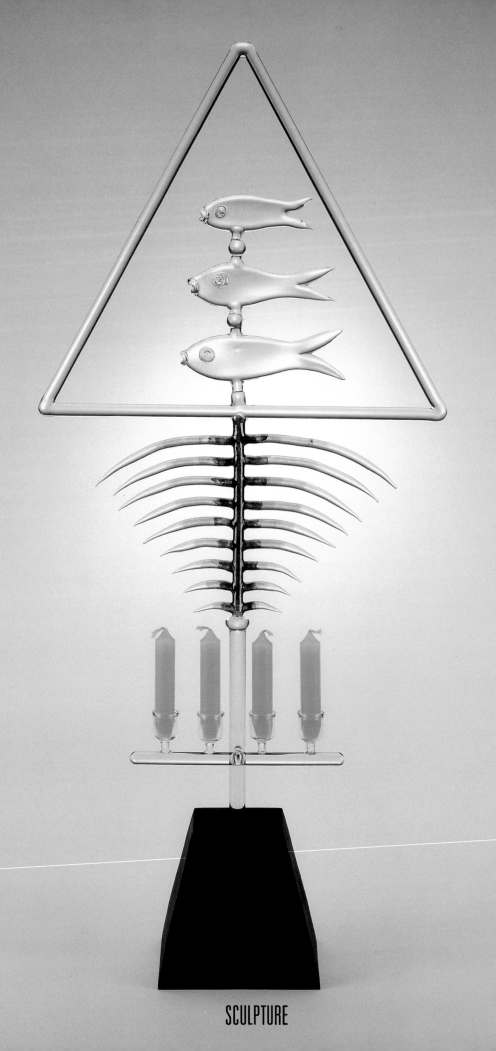

SCULPTURE

Richard Posner
Transparent War Record: Fuck Rambo, *from Pro-American Bandstand*
1986
Blown glass, metal stand
13 x 15 x 10″
Collection of Tom Friedman and Willow Young,
Los Angeles, California

Clifford Rainey
The Intoxication of the Uliad
1986
Cast crystal and plate glass, acid-etched
15¼ x 10 ⁷/₁₆ x 5″
Collection of Dorothy and George Saxe,
Menlo Park, California

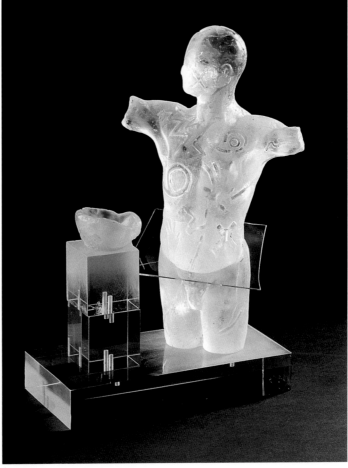

◁ Susan Plum
Retablo: Pescados
1990
Lampworked glass, fired lusters, wood
42 x 17 x 8″
Courtesy of the Artist,
Seattle, Washington

SCULPTURE

Ginny Ruffner
Red Flowers, Floating Back
1991
Lampworked glass, colored
pencil, oil paint
18 x 32 x 14"
Courtesy of the Artist and the
Linda Farris Gallery,
Seattle, Washington

Therman Statom
Seven Years Ago
1986
Sandblasted and painted plate
glass
76½ x 18½ x 4"
Collection of Sonny and Gloria
Kamm, Encino, California

▷Mary Shaffer
Opposite Blue
1980
Slumped glass
42 x 50 x 10"
Courtesy of the Artist and
O.K. Harris Works of Art,
New York, New York

SCULPTURE

SCULPTURE

John Torreano
Gem #3
1990
Blown, cut, and polished glass
11 x 15½ x 11″
Courtesy of the Artist and
the Linda Farris Gallery,
Seattle, Washington

▷ Steven Weinberg
Untitled
1989
Cast crystal, acid-etched and
polished
8⅞ x 8¾ x 8¾″
Collection of Sonny and Gloria
Kamm, Encino, California

Karla Trinkley
Cake
1984
Cast glass, pate de verre
technique
8⅛ x 9⅛ x 9⅞″
Collection of Dorothy
and George Saxe,
Menlo Park, California

Bertil Vallien
The Message
1984
Sandcast glass with copper and
glass inclusions, steel and wire
stand
7¼ x 18¾ x 8¼″
Collection of Kate Elliott,
Seattle, Washington

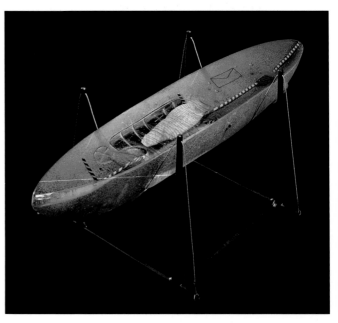

SCULPTURE

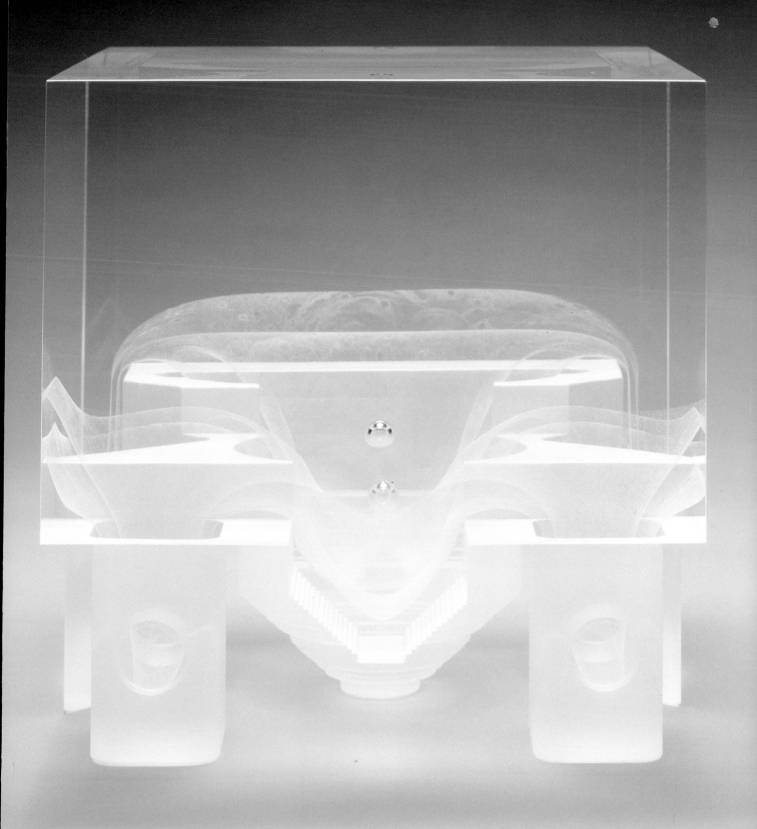

SCULPTURE

Ed Carpenter
Presentation Panel,
commissioned for the
Performing Arts Center,
Anchorage, Alaska
1988
Plate glass, copper, marbles
42 x 36"
Collection of the Artist,
Portland, Oregon

Ed Carpenter
Preliminary Drawing,
commissioned for the
Performing Arts Center,
Anchorage, Alaska
(not illustrated)
1988
Ink on paper
30 x 24"
Collection of the Artist,
Portland, Oregon

Ed Carpenter
Preliminary Drawing,
commissioned for the
Performing Arts Center,
Anchorage, Alaska
(not illustrated)
1988
Graphite on paper
30 x 24"
Collection the Artist,
Portland, Oregon

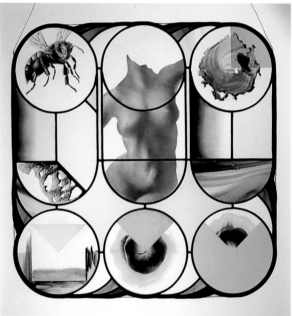

Albinas Elskus
Eve and the Apple
1981
Leaded glass with fired vitrious
paint and silver-stain
26 x 26"
Collection of Sam and Alfreda
Maloof, Alta Loma, California

71

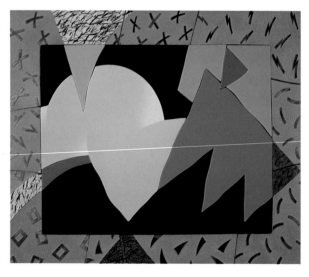

Henry Halem
Untitled
1982
Cut, painted, and sandblasted
Vitrolite, fired enamels
22½ x 27"
Collection of John H. Hauberg,
Seattle, Washington

FLAT GLASS

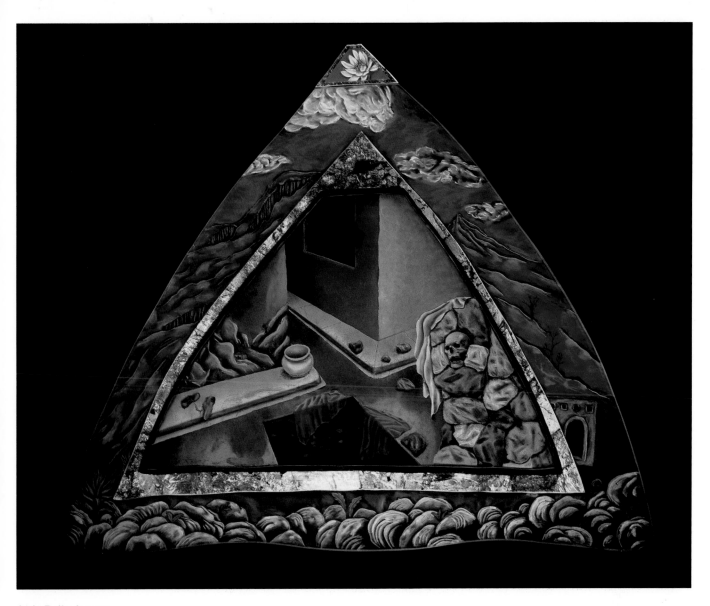

Judy Bally Jensen
Valley of the Kings
1989
Sandblasted and acid-etched
plate glass, acrylic paint, colored
pencil, oil pastels, spray
enamels, wax oils, gold leaf
38 x 45''
Collection of the Artist,
Austin, Texas

FLAT GLASS

FLAT GLASS

Robert Kehlmann
Bay Marsh
1986
Sandblasted and copper brazed
blown glass over acrylic paint
on board
16 x 13″
Courtesy of the Artist and the
Dorothy Weiss Gallery,
San Francisco, California

Narcissus Quagliata
Self-Portrait
1986
Leaded glass
60¼ x 71″
Courtesy of the Artist,
Oakland, California

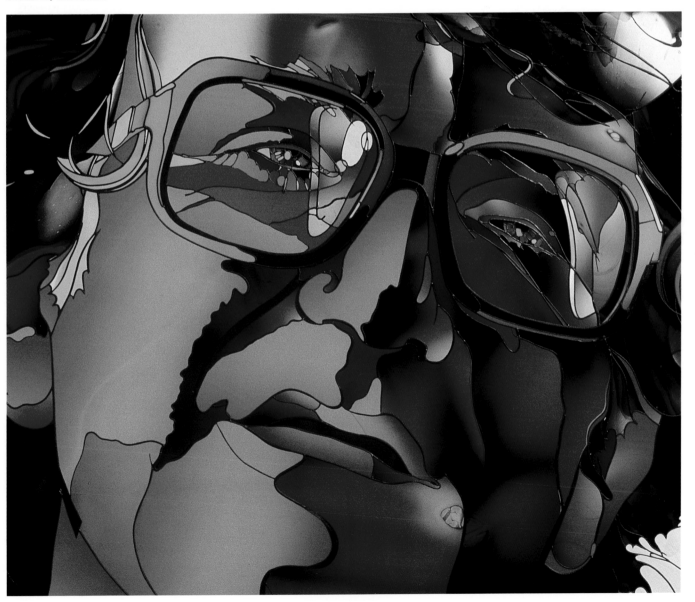

FLAT GLASS

Susan Stinsmuehlen-Amend
X Madonna
1980
Leaded glass, painted thorns,
silicone, plastic figures, lace,
beads, found objects
32 x 25¼"
Collection of the Pilchuck Glass
School, Seattle and
Stanwood, Washington

Patrick Reyntiens, Italo Scanga,
Bob Bailey, and Patrick Clensay
Tree of Life
1978
Leaded glass, fired enamels
30 x 32½"
Collection of the Pilchuck Glass
School, Seattle and
Stanwood, Washington

FLAT GLASS

Laddie John Dill
Untitled
 1990
Monotype on paper
30 x 22″
Collection of the Pilchuck Glass
School, Seattle and
Stanwood, Washington

Roberto Juarez
All Pauls *(not illustrated)*
1991
Monotype on paper
30 x 22″
Collection of the Pilchuck Glass
School, Seattle and
Stanwood, Washington

Liz Mapelli
Cracked Plate *(not illustrated)*
1991
Monotype on paper
22 x 30″
Collection of the Pilchuck Glass
School, Seattle and
Stanwood, Washington

Jan Mares
Karluvmost *(not illustrated)*
1991
Monotype on paper
30 x 22″
Collection of the Pilchuck Glass
School, Seattle and
Stanwood, Washington

GLASS PLATE PRINTS

Italo Scanga and Dale Chihuly
**Abraham and His Only Son,
Isaac**
1991
Monotype on paper
30 x 22"
Collection of the Pilchuck Glass
School, Seattle and
Stanwood, Washington

77

Susan Stinsmuelhlen-Amend
Fluke Studies
1990
Monotype on paper
22 x 30"
Collection of the Pilchuck Glass
School, Seattle and
Stanwood, Washington

GLASS PLATE PRINTS

Wiliam T. Wiley
Mono Man as GR
1990
Monotype on paper
30 x 22″
Collection of the Pilchuck Glass
School, Seattle and
Stanwood, Washington

Hans Gottfried Von Stockhausen
Untitled *(not illustrated)*
1990
Monotype on paper
22 x 15″
Collection of the Pilchuck Glass
School, Seattle and
Stanwood, Washington

GLASS PLATE PRINTS

Endnotes

Introduction

[1] Chloe Zerwick, *A Short History of Glass* (New York: Harry N. Abrams, Inc. 1990), 15.

[2] Ron Glowen, "Glass Art in Washington State: A Brief History," *Artist Trust* (March 1990): 1.

[3] Susanne K. Frantz, *Contemporary Glass* (New York: Harry N. Abrams, Inc., 1989), 35-36.

[4] Glowen, 1.

[5] Harvey K. Littleton, telephone conversation with the author, October 1991.

[6] Dale Chihuly, telephone conversation with the author, October 1991.

[7] Jack Lenor Larsen, conversation with the author, New York, New York, May 1991.

[8] Karen S. Chambers and Jack Cowart, *Chihuly: A Decade of Glass* (Bellevue, Washington: Bellevue Art Museum, 1984), 60.

[9] Ibid.

[10] Dale Chihuly, conversation with the author, Seattle, Washington, July 1991.

[11] Fritz Dreisbach, Kate Elliott, Anne Gould Hauberg and John Landon, group conversation with the author, Seattle, Washington, March 1991.

[12] Chihuly conversation.

[13] Chihuly telephone conversation.

[14] John H. Hauberg, conversation with the author, Seattle, Washington, July 1991.

[15] Ibid.

[16] Group conversation.

[17] Chambers and Cowart, 60.

[18] Hauberg conversation.

Building the School, 1971-77

[1] Ruth Tamura, telephone conversation with the author, September 1991.

[2] Group conversation.

[3] Hauberg conversation.

[4] Group conversation.

[5] Richard Marquis, conversation with the author, Freeland, Washington, May 1991.

[6] Group conversation.

[7] James Carpenter, taped recollections sent to the author, September 1991.

[8] Ibid.

[9] Hauberg conversation.

[10] Tamura telephone conversation.

[11] Ibid.

[12] Louis "Buster" Simpson, conversation with the author, Seattle, Washington, September 1991.

[13] Chihuly telephone conversation.

[14] Simpson conversation.

[15] Hauberg conversation.

[16] Ruth Tamura, "Evaluation for Glass Workshop, UICA Instructional Units 1970/71," (Oakland, California: California College or Arts and Crafts, 31 August 1971), 1.

[17] Ibid.

[18] Hauberg conversation.

[19] Chihuly telephone conversation.

[20] Simpson conversation.

[21] Alice Rooney, telephone conversation with John Olbrantz, June 1992.

[22] Ibid.

[23] Group conversation.

[24] Therman Statom, conversation with the author, Los Angeles, California, August 1991.

[25] Ibid.

[26] Ibid.

[27] Richard Posner, conversation with the author, Los Angeles, California, August 1991.

[28] Hauberg conversation.

[29] C. David Hughbanks, written comments to John Olbrantz, March 1992.

[30] Posner conversation.

[31] Chihuly telephone conversation.

[32] Simpson conversation.

[33] Posner conversation.

[34] "Pilchuck: Two Views," *Glass* 5 (January 1977): 18.

[35] Ibid.

[36] Harvey K. Littleton, letter to the author, January, 1991.

[37] Hauberg conversation.

[38] Thomas Bosworth, "Building Arts: Handbuilt at Pilchuck," *Craft Horizons* 39 (April 1979): 37-38.

[39] Paul Marioni, conversation with the author, Seattle, Washington, July 1991.

Pilchuck and the World, 1978-91

[1] William Morris, conversation with the author, Stanwood, Washington, May 1991.

[2] Statom conversation.

[3] Klaus Moje, conversation with the author, New York, New York, May 1991.

[4] John H. Hauberg, written comments to the author, October 1991.

[5] Alice Rooney, conversation with the author, Seattle, Washington, January 1991.

[6] Hughbanks written comments.

[7] Ibid.

[8] Ibid.

[9] Ibid.

[10] Ibid.

[11] Alice Rooney, letter to the author, October 1991.

[12] Jack Lenor Larsen conversation.

[13] Alice Rooney, conversation with the author, Seattle, Washington, October 1991.

[14] Hauberg conversation.

[15] Hauberg written comments.

[16] Joey Kirkpatrick, conversation with the author, Seattle, Washington, April 1991.

[17] Thomas S. Buechner, conversation with the author, Corning, New York, May 1991.

[18] Carpenter tape.

[19] Ibid.

Bibliography

Ament, Deloris Tarzan. "Bellevue's Pilchuck show offers progress reports on glass art." *Seattle Times/Seattle Post-Intelligencer,* 27 March 1988, sec. L, p. 4.

Anderson, Nola. "Pilchuck - GO." *Craft Australia,* no. 3 (Spring 1986): 114-15.

Aronson, Chris. "Camp Pilchuck." *Glass Studio* 1 (January/February 1978): 12-17.

Aronson, Margery. "Glorious Glass: A Salute to the Pilchuck Glass School." *Glass Art Society Journal* (1990): 33-34.

"At Victoria - Students help revive 'dying' art of glass blowing." *Stanwood (Washington) News,* 7 July 1971, 1.

Bak, Kristine. "Pilchuck, Glass, and Architects." *The Quarterly* (Winter 1980): 6-7.

Bellevue Art Museum. *Pilchuck School: The Great Northwest Glass Experiment.* Bellevue, Washington: Bellevue Art Museum, 1988.

Berger, David. "Pilchuck School shows its works." *Seattle Times Tempo,* 14 December 1984, 16-17.

Bergsman, Jerry. "Pretty Glassy: Center attracts students from around the world." *Seattle Times,* Northern ed., 1 August 1984, sec. F, p. 1.

_____. "Two blaze a trail from Belltown to the Pilchuck Glass Center." *Seattle Times,* Northern ed., 1 August 1984, sec. F, p. 3.

Biskeborn, Susan. "Pilchuck School and the 25-year-old art glass movement." *The (Seattle) Weekly,* 15 July 1987, 33.

Bosworth, Thomas L. "Building Arts: Handbuilt at Pilchuck." *Craft Horizons* 39 (April 1979): 36-38.

_____. "The Pilchuck School, Office/Gallery, Stanwood, Washington, USA." *Architecture and Urbanism,* no. 153 (June 1983): 85-90.

Brewster, Todd. "Avant Glass." *Life,* February 1982, 78-82.

Burley, George. "Unique Glass Center Grows on Hauberg Tree Farm." *Northwest Arts* 2 (20 August 1976): 1.

Campbell, R.M. "The Extraordinary Pilchuck Glass Center." *Seattle Post-Intelligencer,* 9 October 1977, sec. G. p. 6.

_____. "Glass full of energy." *Seattle Post-Intelligencer,* 3 December 1981, sec. D, p. 14.

_____. "The Resurgence In Glass-Making." *Seattle Post-Intelligencer* 206, 20 August 1976, 17.

Carmichael, Suzanne. "The Art of Glass in the Northwest." *New York Times,* 30 December 1990, sec. 5, p. 6.

Chambers, Karen S. *Pilchuck: The Creative Fire.* Olympia, Washington: Washington State Capital Museum, 1986.

_____. "The Pilchuck Story." *New Work* (Winter/Spring 1984): 33-36.

Chambers, Karen S. and Jack Cowart. *Chihuly: A Decade of Glass.* Bellevue, Washington: Bellevue Art Museum, 1984.

Chihuly, Dale. *Chihuly: Color, Glass, and Form.* Forward by Henry Geldzahler. Tokyo, New York, San Francisco: Kodansha International, 1986.

Cohen, Edie Lee. "Art Glass Lamps from the Pilchuck School." *Interior Design* 56 (May 1985): 284-85.

Connell, Joan. "The Fires of Creation." *Bellingham (Washington) Herald Friday Magazine,* 24 July 1981, 8.

Dean, John. "Glass School has worldwide reputation." *Stanwood/Camano (Washington) News,* 22 July 1981, 5.

Ehlers, Jake. "Living and Breathing Glass—Pilchuck Glass Center." *Seattle Madison Park Post,* June 1981, 3.

Fiege, Gale. "Glass blowing among works featured." *Mt. Vernon (Washington) Skagit Valley Herald,* 25 July 1985, sec. 2, p. 17.

Fox, Catherine. "Promising Spirit of Exploration Permeates Pilchuck Glass Exhibit." *Atlanta Journal and Constitution,* 13 June 1989, sec. B, p. 4.

Frantz, Susanne K. *Contemporary Glass.* New York: Harry N. Abrams, Inc., 1989.

Glowen, Ronald. "Glass Art in Washington State: A Brief History." *Artist Trust* (March 1990): 1.

_____. "Glass on the Cutting Edge." *Artweek* 21 (6 December 1990): 25.

_____. *Pilchuck Glass Artists from the American Northwest: An Exhibit of Contemporary Glass Art.* Prague, Czechoslovakia: Embassy, United States of America, 1988.

Gyure, Michelle. "Seattle: The Hot Glass Hot Spot." *Glass Art* 3 (September/October 1988): 4-6.

Hackett, Regina. "Pilchuck glass workers stranded somewhere between craft and art." *Seattle Post-Intelligencer What's Happening,* 12 December 1986, 10.

_____. "Surprising diversity makes strong Pilchuck glass show." *Seattle Post-Intelligencer,* 29 March 1988, sec. C, p. 1.

Houde, Francois. "An Essay on the Pilchuck Glass Center." *Craft News* 6 (May 1981): 1-2.

Haufschild, Lutz. "Pilchuck Glass School - Teaching What Cannot be Taught." *Stained Glass* 78 (Spring 1983): 35-39.

Herber, Christoph. "Von Hadamar nach Pilchuck." *Glas + Rahmen* 38 (2 October 1987): 917-18.

Ingram, Jan. "Skill makes glass a lively medium." *Anchorage Daily News,* 14 November 1981, sec. F, p. 2.

Ives, Rich. "Where Fire Meets Water." *Art and Antiques* (April 1987): 112-15.

Jacobs, Karrie. "Art Glass from the Pilchuck School." *alaskafest,* April 1981, 24-30.

Jarosewitsch, Rena. "The purpose of art...: The Johannes Schreiter experience at Pilchuck Glass School." *New Zealand Crafts* (Autumn 1989): 23-27.

Johns, Linda. "Pilchuck Artists Lend New Dimensions to Art of Glass." *Seattle Argus,* 1 April 1983, 9.

Kendall, Sue Ann. "Pilchuck School's glass artistry: Impressive exhibition here shows versatility in works by many artists." *Seattle Times,* 2 December 1981, sec. F, p. 8.

Losken, M. "From Hadamar to Pilchuck." *Neues Glas,* no 1 (January/March 1988): 42-43.

Manuel, Bruce. "The Glass Blower's Delicate, Demanding Art." *Christian Science Monitor,* 28 June 1989, 10-11.

Mathieson, Karen. "Clear and present; Gallery exhibits around town show sculptors at the head of their glass." *Seattle Times,* 4 April 1991, sec. F, p. 3.

_____ . "Glass Magnets: The creative fires of both glass artist Dale Chihuly and the Pilchuck Glass School draw artists from around the world." *Seattle Times/Seattle Post-Intelligencer,* 18 November 1990, sec. L, p. 1.

_____ . "Like any family, Pilchuck's has its differences." *Seattle Times/ Seattle Post-Intelligencer,* 18 November 1990, sec. L., p. 1.

Miller, Bonnie J. *Out of the Fire: Northwest Glass.* San Francisco: Chronicle Books, 1991.

Mills, Dale Douglas. "Pacific Northwest Living." *Seattle Times Pictorial Magazine,* 15 October 1978, 40-47.

Monaghan, Peter. "A striking campus attracts a rare assembly of artists in glass." *Chronicle of Higher Education* 37 (7 August 1991): A3.

Moody, Fred. "Glass: Northwest artists shatter the plebian image of this blooming aesthetic medium." *Seattle Times/ Seattle Post-Intelligencer Pacific Magazine,* 18 August 1985, 6-10.

Murphy, Jim. "The Pilchuck School, Stanwood, USA." *Architecture and Urbanism,* no. 141 (June 1982): 73-82.

_____ . "Timber and Glass." *Progressive Architecture* 62 (June 1981): 98-101.

Nokkentved, N.S. "Fire & Ice: Heat of Pilchuck's kiln, sweat of its artists produce grace in glass." *Bellingham (Washington) Herald,* 6 September 1987, sec. C, p. 1.

"The Pilchuck Experience: At the Pilchuck School, nothing else exists but the study and creation of glass art." *International Sculpture* 5 (September/October 1986): 41.

"Pilchuck: Two Views." *Glass* 5 (January 1977): 15.

Richardson, Sarah. "Forever Blowing Bubbles: Report from Seattle." *British Artists in Glass Newsletter* (Summer 1986): 35-37.

Robinson, John S. "A Glass Menagerie." *Pacific Northwest,* December 1983, 28-33.

Rooney, Alice. "Two Decades of the Pilchuck Glass School." *Glass Art Society Journal* (1990): 85-87.

Scigliano, Eric. "The Fragile Beauty of Pilchuck Glass." *Seattle Argus,* 14 December 1979, 9.

"Seattle Sights." *Art in America* 74 (July 1986): 68-83.

Segaar, Jim. "Glass Art: Pilchuck School is haven for the masters." *Mt. Vernon (Washington) Skagit Valley Herald,* 18 July 1981, sec. 1, p. 1.

Signor, Randy Michael. "Pilchuck Glass School Celebrates 20 Years." *Crafts Report* 17 (January 1991): 1.

Silberman, Robert. "Will Success Spoil the Glass Art Society?" *American Craft* 50 (August/September 1990): 60-63.

Smallwood, Lyn. "House of glass: fame and fortune in the shadow of Mount Pilchuck." *The (Seattle) Weekly,* 17 August 1983, 43-45.

Tamura, Ruth. "Evaluation for Glass Workshop, UICA Instructional Units 1970/71." Oakland, California: California College of Arts and Crafts, 31 August 1971.

Tarzan, Deloris. "Glass artists don't do windows." *Seattle Times,* 9 April 1981, sec. E, p. 1.

Taylor, Michael. "Glass education in the USA." *Neues Glas,* no. 3 (1989): 232-38.

Tovell, Vincent and Paul de Hueck, prod. *Fire and Sand: the Mysteries of Glass.* 56 min., Canadian Broadcasting Corporation, 1981.

Tsutakawa, Mayumi. "Glassblowers hardy breed." *Seattle Times,* 10 September 1978, sec. M, p. 1.

_____ . "Glassblowing is fragile art, but the people aren't." *Seattle Times,* 10 September 1978, sec. M, p. 6.

"U.S. Workshop of the Year: Pilchuck Glass Center." *Craft Horizons* 34 (April 1974): 41.

Vilmanis, Velta. "Pilchuck '87." *Ausglass Magazine* (Spring 1987): 13.

Von Schack, Katherine. "Glass comes into its own." *Vancouver,* November 1981, 61-69.

Waite, Stephen K. "Welcome to Pilchuck." *Bellevue (Washington) Daily Journal American AM/PM,* 20 August 1976, 7.

Wellings, Marjorie. "Pilchuck glass has glowing reputation." *Davis (California) Enterprise Weekend,* 24 October 1985, 10-11.

Zerwick, Chloe. *A Short History of Glass.* New York: Harry N. Abrams, Inc., 1990.

Appendix

Pilchuck Glass School faculty, visiting artists (VA) and artists-in-residence (AR), 1971-91. Compiled by the Pilchuck Glass School, Seattle and Stanwood, Washington.

1971
James Carpenter
Dale Chihuly
John Landon
Buster Simpson
Ruth Tamura
Art Wood - VA

1972
John Benson
James Carpenter
Dale Chihuly
Fritz Dreisbach
Erwin Eisch
Doug Hollis
John Landon
Robert Naess
Buster Simpson
Stan Vanderbeek
Art Wood

1973
Harry Anderson
James Carpenter
Dale Chihuly
Fritz Dreisbach
Italo Scanga
Buster Simpson

1974
Rob Adamson
Dale Chihuly
Fritz Dreisbach
Rob Levin
Marvin Lipofsky
Harvey Littleton
Paul Marioni

1975
James Carpenter
Fritz Dreisbach
Paul Marioni
Mark Peiser
Jack Schmidt

1976
James Carpenter
Dale Chihuly
Dan Dailey
Fritz Dreisbach
Seaver Leslie
Paul Marioni
Italo Scanga
Jack Schmidt

1977
James Carpenter
Dale Chihuly
Dan Dailey
Fritz Dreisbach
Paul Marioni
Italo Scanga
Ludwig Schaffrath

1978
Dale Chihuly
Michael Cohn
Dan Dailey
Roger Ek
Robert Kehlmann
Harvey Littleton
Patrick Reyntiens
Jerry Rhodes
Italo Scanga
Ludwig Schaffrath
Bud Schorr

1979
Dale Chihuly
Brian Clarke
Dan Dailey
Fritz Dreisbach
Richard Marquis
Isgard Moje *(now Moje-Wohlgemuth)*
Klaus Moje
Benjamin Moore
Patrick Reyntiens
Italo Scanga
Ludwig Schaffrath
Ann Warff *(now Wolff)*

1980
William Bernstein
Dale Chihuly
Dan Dailey
Fritz Dreisbach
Albinas Elskus
Ulrica Hydman-Vallien
Robert Kehlmann
Harvey Littleton
Paul Marioni
Joel Phillip Myers
Klaus Moje
Benjamin Moore
Richard Posner
Narcissus Quagliata
Italo Scanga
Mary Shaffer—AR
Ludwig Schaffrath
Robert Strini—AR
Lino Tagliapietra—AR
Bertil Vallien

1981
Thomas Buechner—VA
James Carpenter
Dale Chihuly—AR
Dan Dailey
Erwin Eisch
Albinas Elskus
Erik Hogland
James Houston—VA
Ulrica Hydman-Vallien
Joey Kirkpatrick
Marvin Lipofsky—VA
Harvey Littleton—AR
Flora Mace
Paul Marioni
Klaus Moje
Narcissus Quagliata
Italo Scanga—AR
Johannes Schreiter
Therman Statom—VA
Susan Stinsmuehlen
(now Stinsmuehlen-Amend)—AR
Bertil Vallien
William Warmus—VA
Dick Weiss—VA

1982
Jaroslava Brychtova—AR
Thomas Buechner—AR
Dale Chihuly—AR
Dan Dailey
Fritz Dreisbach—AR
Albinas Elskus
Michael Glancy
Henry Halem
James Harmon—AR
Richard Harned
Ulrica Hydman-Vallien
Margie Jervis—AR
Ray King
Joey Kirkpatrick
Susie Krasnican
Stanislav Libensky—AR
Finn Lynngaard
Flora Mace
Linda MacNeil

Klaus Moje
Jochem Poensgen
Carl Powell
Susan Stinsmuehlen
(now Stinsmuehlen-Amend)
Barbara Vaessen
Bertil Vallien
Dick Weiss—AR
Toots Zynsky—AR

1983
Mary Ann Babula
Jaroslava Brychtova—AR
Thomas Buechner—AR
William Carlson
Bruce Chao—AR
Dale Chihuly—AR
Jon Clark
Erwin Eisch
Margarete Eisch
Albinas Elskus
Michael Glancy
Henry Halem
David Huchthausen
Joey Kirkpatrick
Stanislav Libensky—AR
Flora Mace
Richard Meitner
Pavel Molnar
Jochem Poensgen
Narcissus Quagliata
Italo Scanga—AR
Susan Stinsmuehlen
(now Stinsmuehlen-Amend)
Lino Tagliapietra—AR
Barbara Vaessen
Bertil Vallien
Bertil Vallien—AR
Dick Weiss
Dana Zamecnikova—AR

1984
Lynda Benglis—AR
Rich Bernstein
Thomas Buechner—AR
Kathie Bunnell
Ed Carpenter
Karen Chambers—AR
Michael Cohn
Bill Concannon—AR
Sheryl Cotleur
Dan Dailey
Fritz Dreisbach
Erwin Eisch
Katherine Eisch
Michael Glancy
Ulrica Hydman-Vallien
Margie Jervis
Michael Kennedy—AR
Sheila Klein—AR
Susie Krasnican
Marvin Lipofsky
Paul Marioni
Richard Marquis
Nancy Mee—AR
Tim O'Neill
Jerry Pethick—AR
Carl Powell
Narcissus Quagliata
Clifford Rainey
Ginny Ruffner
Therman Statom
Molly Stone
Cappy Thompson—AR
John Torreano—AR
Bertil Vallien
Ann Warff *(now Wolff)*
Dick Weiss—AR
Mary White
Chris Wilmarth—AR
Toots Zynsky

1985
Larry Ahvakana
Lynda Benglis—AR
Sonja Blomdahl
Ruth Brockman
William Carlson
Ed Carpenter
Dale Chihuly—AR
Dan Dailey
Fritz Dreisbach—AR
Albinas Elskus
Ann Gardner—AR
Michael Glancy
Jiri Harcuba
Lutz Haufschild
Robert Kehlmann—AR
Joachim Klos
Rick LaLonde
Andrew Magdanz
Paul Marioni—AR
Richard Marquis
Jay Musler
Robert Naess—AR
Judy North
Tim O'Neill
Richard Posner—AR
Clifford Rainey
Jan Erik Ritzman
Amy Roberts
Ginny Ruffner
Norie Sato—AR
Italo Scanga—AR
Susan Shapiro
Debra Sherwood—AR
Therman Statom
Susan Stinsmuehlen
(now Stinsmuehlen-Amend)
Lino Tagliapietra
Fred Tschida
Barbara Vaessen—AR
Bertil Vallien
Bert VanLoo
William Warmus
Steven Weinberg
Dana Zamecnikova

1986
Channa Bankier
Howard Ben Tre—AR
Joan Ross Bloedel—AR
Jaroslava Brychtova
Thomas Buechner—AR
Sydney Cash
Dale Chihuly—AR
Norman Courtney
Paulo DuFour
Erwin Eisch
Kate Elliot
Albinas Elskus
Michael Glancy
Henry Halem
Jiri Harcuba
Richard Harned—AR
Robert Hodges—AR
Eric Hopkins—AR
David Huchthausen—AR
Ulrica Hydman-Vallien
Diane Katsiaficas—AR
Joey Kirkpatrick
Warren Langley
Stanislav Libensky
Flora Mace
Paul Marioni
Klaus Moje
Louis Mueller—AR
Joel Phillip Myers
Ron Onoroto—AR
Charles Parriott
Jerry Pethick—AR
Jan Erik Ritzman
Ginny Ruffner
Italo Scanga—AR

Peter Shire—AR
Therman Statom
Susan Stinsmuehlen
(now Stinsmuehlen-Amend)
Fred Tschida
Bertil Vallien
Hans Gottfried Von Stockhausen
William Warmus
Ed Wicklander—AR
Ann Wolff

1987
Walter Darby Bannard—VA
Dorit Brand
Jaroslava Brychtova
Tom Buechner—AR
Kathie Bunnell
Anna Carlgren—AR
Dale Chihuly
Dale Chihuly—AR
KeKe Cribbs
Dan Dailey—AR
William Dexter
Albinas Elskus—AR
Kate Elliott
Jiri Harcuba
James Harmon
David Hopper
Diana Hobson
Ursula Huth—AR
Joey Kirkpatrick
Joey Kirkpatrick—AR
Stanislav Libensky
Walter Lieberman—AR
Harvey Littleton
Flora Mace
Flora Mace—AR
Andrew Magdanz
Paul Marioni
Maxine Martell—AR
Lucy Mohl—AR
Klaus Moje
Benjamin Moore
William Morris—AR
Judy North
Danny Perkins—AR
Narcissus Quagliata
Amy Roberts
Ginny Ruffner
Italo Scanga—AR
Susan Shapiro
Susan Stinsmuehlen
(now Stinsmuehlen-Amend)
Jiri Suhajek
Lino Tagliapietra
John Torreano—AR
Karla Trinkley
Fred Tschida
Durk Valkema—AR
Sybren Valkema—AR
Patrick Wadley
William Warmus
David Wharton

1988
Nicholas Africano—AR
Kathie Bunnell
Deborah Dohne—VA
Fritz Dreisbach
Ann Gardner—VA
Michael Glancy
Henry Halem
Jiri Harcuba
Ulrica Hydman-Vallien
Diana Hobson
Andrew Keating—AR
Joey Kirkpatrick
Warren Langley
John Leighton
Marvin Lipofsky
Flora Mace
Liz Mapelli

Paul Marioni
William Morris
Judy North
Ronald Pennell
Jerry Pethick—AR
Pike Powers—AR
Clifford Rainey
Dina Rosin
Loredano Rosin
Ginny Ruffner
Italo Scanga—AR
Ludwig Schaffrath
Johannes Schreiter
Dan Schwoerer
Paul Stankard
Cappy Thompson
John Torreano—AR
Fred Tschida
Fred Tschida—VA
Bertil Vallien
Patrick Wadley
Mary White
Bill Woodrow—VA

1989
Nicholas Africano—AR
Jaroslava Brychtova
Marsha Burns—AR
Michael Burns—AR
Robert Carlson
Jose Chardiet
KeKe Cribbs
Paulo Dufour
Henry Halem
Jiri Harcuba
Diana Hobson
David Hopper
David Huchthausen
Lawrence Jasse
Marian Karel
Joey Kirkpatrick
Stanislav Libensky
Walter Lieberman
Flora Mace
Rachel Mesrahi
William Morris
Judy North
Dennis Oppenheim—AR
Charles Parriott
Judy Pfaff—AR
Pike Powers
Clifford Rainey
Amy Roberts
Richard Royal
Ginny Ruffner
Italo Scanga—AR
Mary Shaffer
Pino Signoretto
Therman Statom
Susan Stinsmuehlen-Amend
Cappy Thompson
John Torreano—AR
Fred Tschida
Bertil Vallien
Robin Winters—AR
Ann Wahlstrom
David Wharton
Bill Woodrow—AR
Dana Zamecnikova

1990
Michele Blondel—AR
Nancy Bowen—AR
Jaroslava Brychtova
Robert Carlson
Jose Chardiet
Dan Dailey
Laddie John Dill—AR
James Drake—AR
Henry Halem
Joey Kirkpatrick
Susie Krasnican

Stanislav Libensky
Donald Lipski—AR
Flora Mace
Liz Mapelli
Jan Mares
Dante Marioni
Tom Marioni—AR
Klaus Moje
William Morris
Dennis Oppenheimn—AR
Mark Peiser
Judy Pfaff—AR
Susam Plum
Amy Roberts
Richard Royal
Ginny Ruffner
Italo Scanga—AR
Michael Scheiner
Henner Schroder
Barbara Schwartz—AR
Pino Signoretto
Paul Stankard
Susan Stinsmuehlen-Amend
John Torreano—AR
Fred Tschida
Hans Gottfried Von Stockhausen
William T. Wiley—AR

1991
Terry Allen—AR
Arlon Bayliss
Curtiss Brock
Dale Chihuly
Bill Concannon
James Drake—AR
Ann Hamilton—AR
Diana Hobson
Judy Bally Jensen
Roberto Juarez—AR
Mark Kobasz
Warren Langley
John Lewis
Donald Lipski—AR
Jan Mares
Dante Marioni
Joseph Marioni—AR
Richard Marquis
Izhar Patkin—AR
Judy Pfaff—AR
Susan Plum
Damian Prior
Narcissus Quagliata
Clifford Rainey
David Reekie
Patrick Reyntiens
Jane Rosen—AR
Loredano Rosin
Cesare Toffolo Rossit
Henner Schroder
Louis Sclafani
Kiki Smith—AR
Susan Stinsmuehlen-Amend
Lino Tagliapietra
Thomas Tisch
Fred Tschida
Kurt Wallstab
William Warmus
James Watkins
Hiroshi Yamano

83

Photo Credits

Jindrich Brok: 59-60
Dick Busher: 19, 30
Ed Carpenter: 71
Dale Chihuly: 11, 12, 13
Ed Claycomb: 15, 24, 75
Susie Cushner: 58
Gail Davis: 7
James Dee: 29
Rod del Pozo: 26, 29, 31, 44, 45, 46, 47,
49, 50, 51, 61, 63, 75, 76, 77, 78
Gene Dwiggins: 44
Albinas Elskus: 71
George Erml: 62, 66, 68
M. Lee Fatherree: 32, 56, 69, 74
Jack Fulton: 33
Galerie Yvon Lambert: 64
Claire Garoutte: 50, 57
Nick Gunderson:1, 9
Henry Halem: 71
Art Hupy: 27
Russell Johnson: 59
John Littleton: 28, 32
Richard Marquis: 45
Glen Millward: 58
Klaus Moje: 45
Ric Murray: 54
Mark Packo: 33
Pilchuck Glass School: 3, 21, 23, 27,
40, 42
Jack Ramsdale: 34
Richard Sargent: 73
Doug Schaible: 56
Roger Schreiber: Cover, 17, 22, 31, 35,
43, 51, 52, 61, 69
Mike Seidl: 66, 67
Rob Vinnedge: 6, 44, 55, 64, 65, 69
Emil Vogely: 72
Ken Yamaguchi: 31, 47-48, 53, 67, 70
Toots Zynsky: 53